Using and Understanding Maps

Rocks and Minerals of the World

Consulting Editor
Scott E. Morris
College of Mines and Earth Resources
University of Idaho

Chelsea House Publishers
New York   Philadelphia

This Publication was designed, edited and computer generated by
Lovell Johns Limited
10 Hanborough Business Park
Long Hanborough
Witney
Oxon, England OX8 8LH

The contents of this volume are based on the latest data available at the
time of publication.

Map credit: *Antarctica source map prepared at 1:20,000 by the British
Antarctic Survey Mapping and Geographic Information Centre, 1990.*

Cover credit: *Harold and Erica Van Pelt, Photographers, Los Angeles.*

Printed in Mexico

First printing

1 3 5 7 9 8 6 4 2

Library of Congress Cataloging in Publication Data

Rocks and minerals of the world/editorial consultant, Scott Morris:
     p. cm. (Using and understanding maps)
     Includes glossary and index/gazetteer.
     Includes bibliographical references.
     Summary: Eighteen map spreads present information about the
     world's geology, minerals, and fossil fuels.
     ISBN 0-7910-1803-2. ISBN 0-7910-1816-4 (pbk.)
1. Minerals — Maps. 2. Rocks — Maps.
[1. Minerals — Maps. 2. Rocks — Maps. 3. Atlases.]
     I. Morris, Scott Edward. II. Chelsea House Publishers. III. Series.
     G1046.H1R6 1993 <G&M>
     552' .0022' 3 — dc20   92-22910
                                         CIP
                                         MAP AC

Introduction

We inhabit a fascinating and mysterious planet where the earth's physical features, life-forms, and the diversity of human culture conspire to produce a breathtaking environment. We don't have to travel very far to see and experience the wealth of this diverse planet; in fact, we don't have to travel at all. Everywhere images of the world are abundantly available in books, newspapers, magazines, movies, television, and the arts. We could say that *everywhere* one looks, our world is a brilliant moving tapestry of shapes, colors, and textures, and our experience of its many messages — whether in our travels or simply by gazing out into our own backyards — is what we call reality.

Geography is the study of a portion of that reality. More so, it is the study of how the physical and biological components (rocks, animals, plants, and people) of our planet are distributed and how they are interconnected. Geographers seek to describe and to explain the physical patterns that have evolved on the earth and also to discover the significance in the ways they have evolved. To do this, geographers rely on maps.

Maps can be powerful images. They convey selective information about vast areas of an overwhelmingly cluttered world. The cartographer, or mapmaker, must carefully choose the theme of a map, that is, what it will show, knowing that a good map will convey the essence of information while at the same time making the information easy to comprehend.

This volume and its companions in UNDERSTANDING AND USING MAPS are about the planet we call earth and the maps we use to find our way along its peaks and valleys. Each volume displays map images that reveal how the world is arranged according to a specific theme such as population, industries or the endangered world. The maps in each volume are accompanied by an interesting collection of facts — some are rather obvious, others are oddities. Yet all are meant to be informative.

Along with a wealth of facts, there are explanations of the various attributes and phenomena depicted by the maps. This information is provided to better understand the significance of the maps as well as to demonstrate how the many themes relate.

Names for places are essential to geographers. To study the world without devising names for places would be extremely difficult. But geographers also know that names are in no way permanent; place names change as people change. The recent reunification of Germany and the breakup of what was the Soviet Union — events that seem colossal from the perspective of socioeconomics — to geographers are simply events that require the drawing or erasing of one or a few boundaries and the renaming of one or several land masses. The geographer is constantly reminded that the world is in flux; a map is always in danger of being rendered obsolete by a turn in current events.

Because the world is dynamic, it continues to captivate the mind and stimulate the imagination. USING AND UNDERSTANDING MAPS presents the world as it is today, with the reservation that any dramatic rearrangement of land and people is likely, indeed inevitable, thus requiring the making of a new map. In this way maps are themselves a part of the evolutionary process.

Scott E. Morris

Rocks and Minerals of the World

A rock is usually an assemblage of minerals. There are more than 1,000 different minerals making up the rocks of our planet, but many of these minerals are extremely rare. In fact, eight elements account for approximately 98 percent of the rocks one is likely to encounter on the earth.

Rocks are classified into three major groups: igneous, sedimentary, and metamorphic.

Igneous rocks are composed of minerals that crystallize from "melts." The eruption of lava from a volcano will create an igneous rock (most often basalt) when it cools.

Sedimentary rocks are, as the name suggests, those composed of sediments. They are formed by compaction of sand, clay, and other materials. Sandstones, shales, and limestones are the most common sedimentary rocks.

Metamorphic rocks are igneous or sedimentary rocks that have been transformed by heat and pressure; the minerals have been altered and rearranged into different forms. Thus sandstone becomes quartzite, shale becomes slate, and limestone becomes marble.

When people think about minerals, they usually think about the so-called precious ones, such as gold, silver, diamonds, and rubies. The worth of a mineral depends not only upon its abundance but also upon its properties. Diamond is the hardest mineral, and its durability, coupled with its attractiveness when skillfully cut, establishes its great value. Gold, on the other hand, is a soft mineral that can be easily worked into different shapes. This property, combined with its metallic luster and its scarcity, is what makes gold desireable and expensive.

Many minerals are rather ordinary looking, but they can also be valuable. Sand, the common building material, is usually composed of quartz, a medium-hard material found in abundance. Iron and aluminium minerals are also plentiful.

If you think of the rocks and minerals of the earth as permanent, you are correct from one perspective yet mistaken from another. In terms of a person's lifetime, the existing mineral wealth of the planet can be exhausted, and there may be considerable environmental costs involved in extraction and processing. Therefore it is important for us to manage our mineral resources wisely and to embrace recycling programs where they are feasible.

On another level, that of *geologic time*, the earth does its own recycling, and minerals are continually being created by various means — even in your backyard as water moves through soil and causes chemical reactions.

The earth is a closed system with respect to rocks and minerals, and the elements are continually being rearranged by processes taking place far below the surface.

Scott E. Morris

legend lists and explains the symbols and colors ed on the map. It is called a legend because it lls the story of a map. It is important to read the ap legend to find out exactly what the symbols ean because some symbols do not look like hat they represent. For example, a dot stands r a town.

very map in this atlas has a legend on it.

This legend lists and explains the colors and symbols used on the map on that page only. The legend on the left, below, shows examples of the colors used on the maps in all the atlases in this series. Below this is a list of all symbols used on the maps in all the atlases in this series.

The legend on the right, below, is an example of a legend used in the physical atlas.

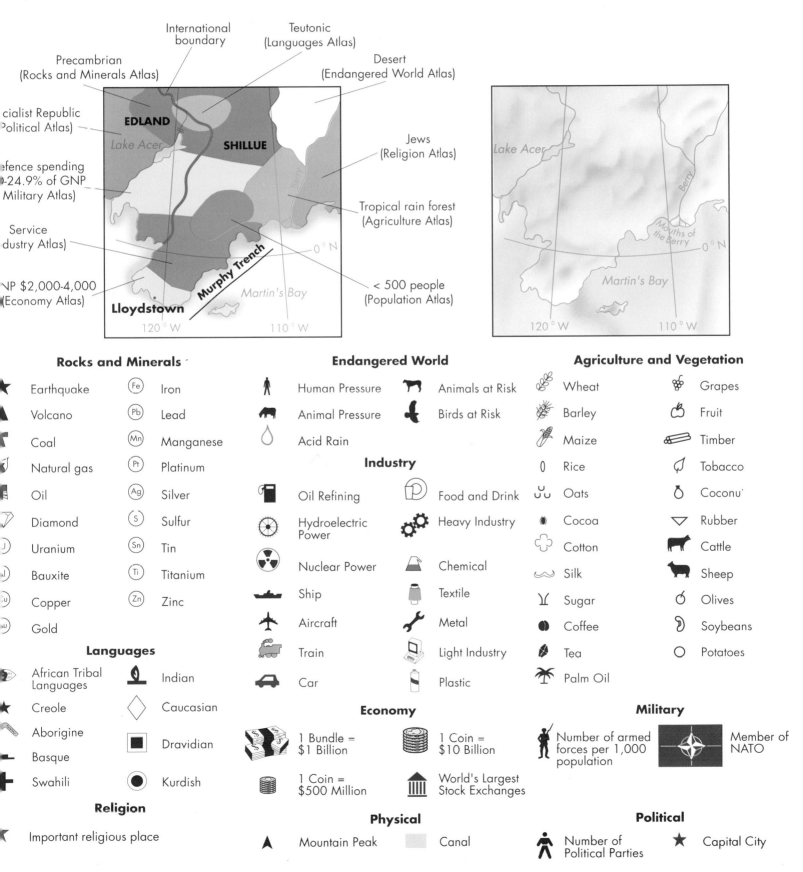

Rocks and Minerals

★	Earthquake	Fe	Iron
▲	Volcano	Pb	Lead
	Coal	Mn	Manganese
	Natural gas	Pt	Platinum
	Oil	Ag	Silver
	Diamond	S	Sulfur
	Uranium	Sn	Tin
	Bauxite	Ti	Titanium
	Copper	Zn	Zinc
	Gold		

Languages

	African Tribal Languages	♨	Indian
★	Creole	◇	Caucasian
	Aborigine	■	Dravidian
	Basque		
	Swahili	●	Kurdish

Religion

☨	Important religious place

Endangered World

🧍	Human Pressure	🐄	Animals at Risk
🐄	Animal Pressure	🦅	Birds at Risk
💧	Acid Rain		

Industry

⛽	Oil Refining	💊	Food and Drink
⚙	Hydroelectric Power	⚙	Heavy Industry
☢	Nuclear Power	⚗	Chemical
🚢	Ship	🧴	Textile
✈	Aircraft	🔧	Metal
🚂	Train	💻	Light Industry
🚗	Car	🧴	Plastic

Economy

💵	1 Bundle = $1 Billion	🪙	1 Coin = $10 Billion
🪙	1 Coin = $500 Million	🏛	World's Largest Stock Exchanges

Physical

▲	Mountain Peak		Canal

Agriculture and Vegetation

🌾	Wheat	🍇	Grapes
🌾	Barley	🍎	Fruit
🌽	Maize		Timber
	Rice		Tobacco
∪∪	Oats		Coconut
●	Cocoa	▽	Rubber
❁	Cotton	🐄	Cattle
∽	Silk	🐑	Sheep
Y	Sugar	◔	Olives
●	Coffee	♪	Soybeans
❦	Tea	○	Potatoes
🌴	Palm Oil		

Military

🪖	Number of armed forces per 1,000 population	✴	Member of NATO

Political

🧍	Number of Political Parties	★	Capital City

World Physical

This page is a physical map of the world. It indicates where the major physical features — such as mountain ranges, plains, deserts, lakes, and rivers — are in the world. As the world is very large, the map has to be drawn at a very small scale in order to fit onto a page. This map is drawn at a scale so that 1 inch on the map, at the equator, equals 1,840 miles on the ground.

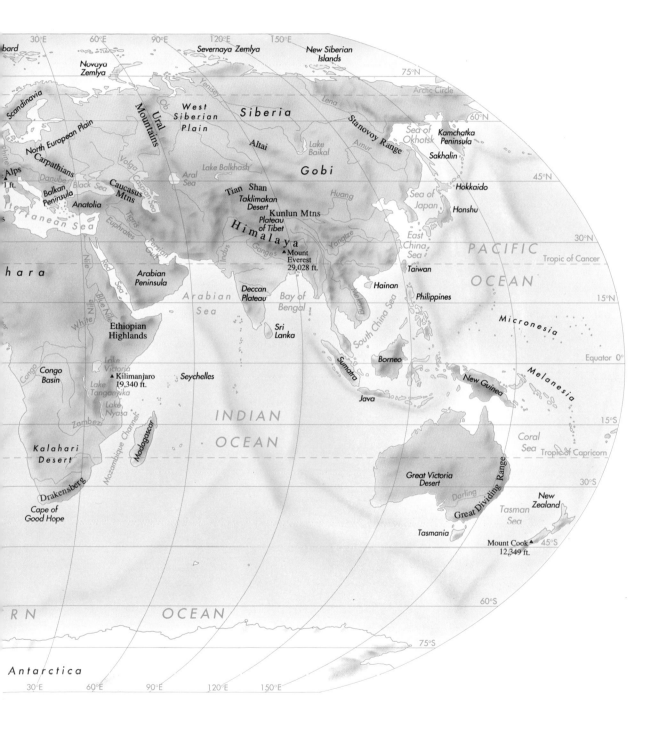

bard

Novaya
Zemlya

Scandinavia

Severnaya Zemlya

New Siberian
Islands

75°N

Arctic Circle

West
Siberian
Plain

Siberia

60°N

North European Plain

Ural
Mountains

Ob

Yenisey

Lena

Stanovoy Range

Amur

Sea of
Okhotsk

Kamchatka
Peninsula

Carpathians

Alps

1 ft.

Volga

Altai

Lake
Baikal

Sakhalin

Danube

Black Sea

Caspian Sea

Aral
Sea

Lake Balkhash

Gobi

45°N

Balkan
Peninsula

Caucasus
Mtns

Anatolia

Tigris

Tian   Shan
Taklimakan
Desert

Huang

Sea of
Japan

Hokkaido

Honshu

terranean Sea

Euphrates

Kunlun Mtns
Plateau
of Tibet

Persian Gulf

Himalaya

Nile

Red Sea

Indus

Ganges

Yangtze

▲Mount
Everest
29,028 ft.

East
China
Sea

PACIFIC

30°N

hara

Arabian
Peninsula

Mount
Everest
29,028 ft.

Tropic of Cancer

Deccan
Plateau

Arabian

Sea

Bay of
Bengal

Mekong

Hainan

Taiwan

Philippines

OCEAN

15°N

Blue Nile

White

Ethiopian
Highlands

Sri
Lanka

South China Sea

Micronesia

Congo

Congo
Basin

Lake
Victoria

▲Kilimanjaro
19,340 ft.

Seychelles

Sumatra

Borneo

Equator 0°

Lake
Tanganyika

Java

New Guinea

Melanesia

15°S

Lake
Nyasa

INDIAN

Zambezi

Mozambique Channel

Madagascar

OCEAN

Coral
Sea

Kalahari
Desert

Great Victoria
Desert

Great Dividing Range

Tropic of Capricorn

30°S

Drakensberg

Darling

New
Zealand

Cape of
Good Hope

Tasman
Sea

Great Dividing Range

Tasmania

Mount Cook▲
12,349 ft.

45°S

60°S

RN

OCEAN

75°S

Antarctica

30°E   60°E   90°E   120°E   150°E

Africa, Northern 10-11

Algeria
Benin
Burkina Faso
Cameroon
Cape Verde
Central African Republic
Chad
Djibouti
Egypt
Ethiopia
Gambia
Ghana
Guinea
Guinea-Bissau
Ivory Coast
Liberia
Libya
Mali
Mauritania
Morocco
Niger
Nigeria
Senegal
Sierra Leone
Somalia
Sudan
Togo
Tunisia
Western Sahara

Africa, Southern 12-13

Angola
Botswana
Burundi
Comoros
Congo
Equatorial Guinea
Gabon
Kenya
Lesotho
Madagascar
Malawi
Mauritius
Mozambique
Namibia
Rwanda

São Tomé & Príncipe
Seychelles
South Africa
Swaziland
Tanzania
Uganda
Zaire
Zambia
Zimbabwe

America, Central 14-15

Antigua & Barbuda
Bahamas
Barbados
Belize
Costa Rica
Cuba
Dominica

Dominican Republic
El Salvador
Grenada
Guatemala
Haiti
Honduras
Jamaica

Mexico
Nicaragua
Panama
St Kitts - Nevis
St Lucia
St Vincent
Trinidad & Tobago

Canada 26-27

Canada

Commonwealth of Independent States 28-29

Armenia
Azerbaijan
Estonia
Georgia
Kazakhstan
Kirghizstan
Latvia
Lithuania
Moldova
Russian Federation

Tajikistan
Turkmenistan
Ukraine
Uzbekhistan

Europe 30-31

Albania
Bosnia & Herzegovina
Bulgaria
Croatia
Czechoslovakia
Finland
Greece
Hungary
Iceland
Norway

Poland
Romania
Slovenia
Sweden
Yugoslavia

Europe, Western 32-33

Andorra
Austria
Belgium
Denmark
France
Germany
Ireland
Italy
Liechtenstein
Luxembourg

Malta
Monaco
Netherlands
Portugal
San Marino
Spain
Switzerland
United Kingdom
Vatican City

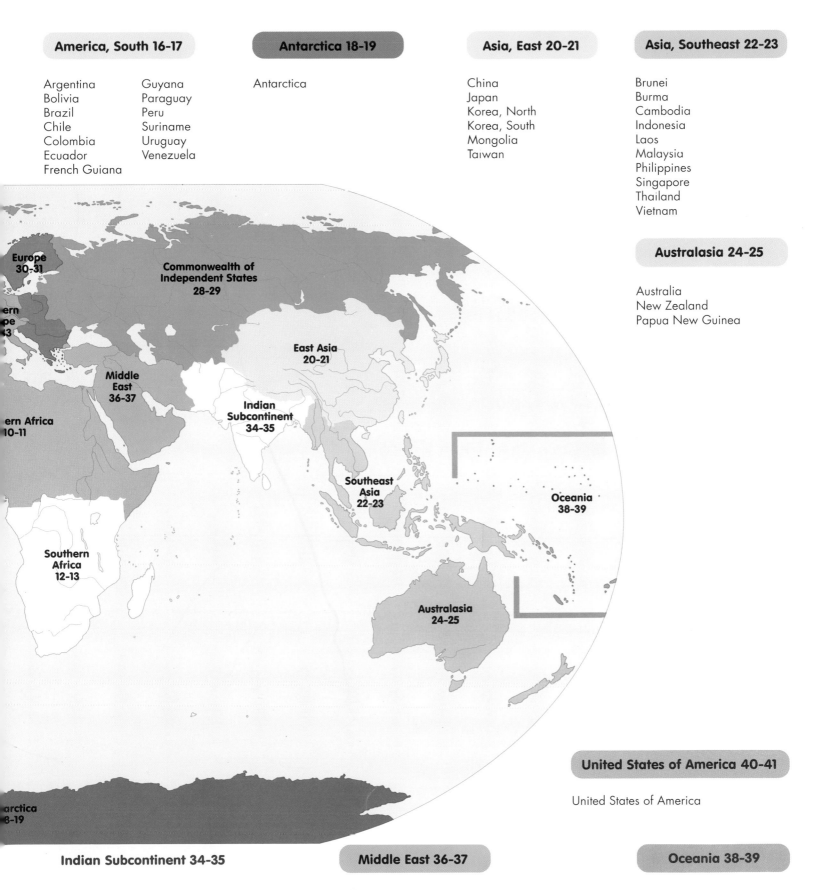

Africa, Northern

Northern Africa is composed largely of ancient, Precambrian rock dating back to the beginning of life on Earth, overlaid with a hugely varying surface. This ranges from vast, arid desert to impenetrable jungles and swamps. Most of the Sahara, the world's biggest desert, consists not of sand but bare rock.

? Did You Know

★ Fossils tell us that the first elephants were only the size of sheep and were about 100 times smaller than today's African elephant.

What the colors and symbols mean

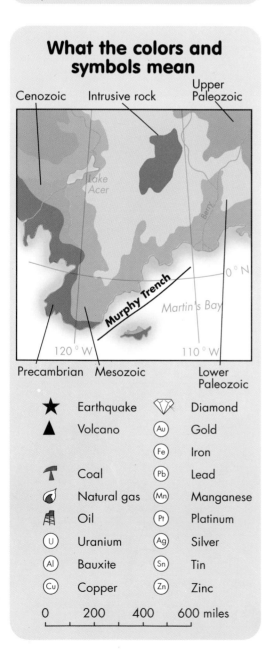

Cenozoic Intrusive rock Upper Paleozoic

Lake Acer

Berry

Murphy Trench

Martin's Bay

120° W   110° W

Precambrian Mesozoic Lower Paleozoic

★	Earthquake	◇	Diamond
▲	Volcano	Au	Gold
		Fe	Iron
⛏	Coal	Pb	Lead
💧	Natural gas	Mn	Manganese
🛢	Oil	Pt	Platinum
U	Uranium	Ag	Silver
Al	Bauxite	Sn	Tin
Cu	Copper	Zn	Zinc

0   200   400   600 miles

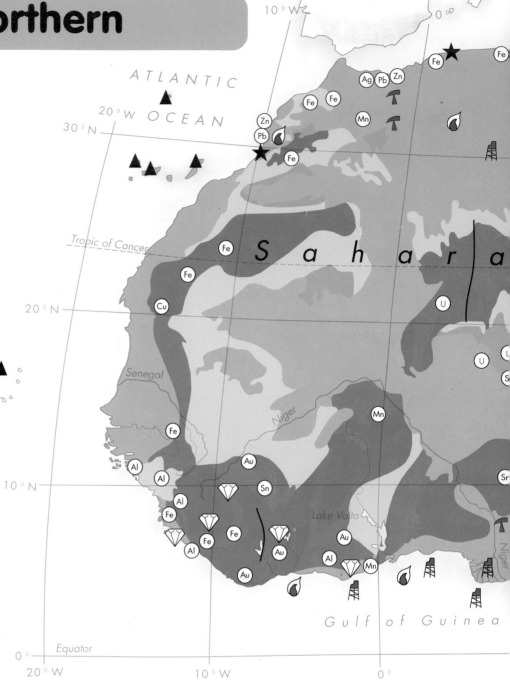

ATLANTIC OCEAN

Tropic of Cancer

Sahara

Senegal   Niger   Lake Volta

Niger

Gulf of Guinea

Equator

20° W   10° W   0°

The diagram below shows a slice of the Earth so that you can see inside. The structure of the Earth is like that of an apple. The skin of the Earth is called the crust. Underneath the crust is a thick layer like the flesh of an apple. This is known as the mantle. At the center of both the apple and the Earth is the core.

Core: This is too deep inside the Earth for scientists to examine. But they think the core has two parts.
Outer core: About 1,200 miles thick. Probably a liquid of molten iron and nickel.
Inner core: About 746 miles in radius. Probably a solid ball of hot metal made up of iron and nickel. Temperature 6,000 – 7,000°F.

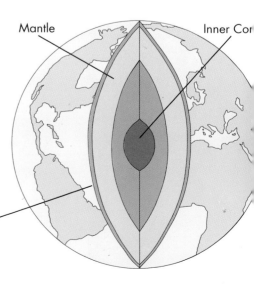

Mantle   Inner Core

Outer Core   Crust

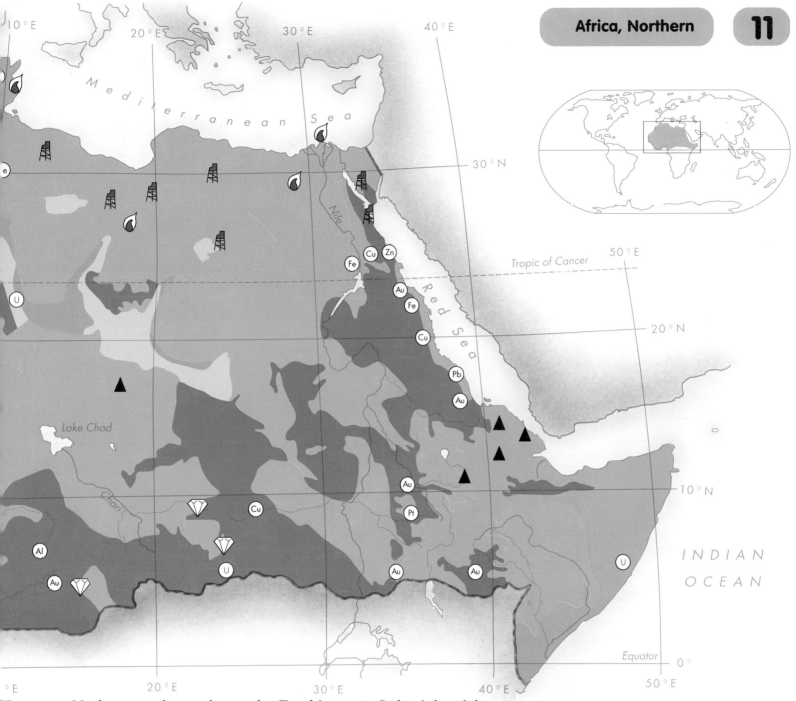

There are 92 elements that make up the Earth's crust. Only eight of these elements are common minerals, but they make up 99% of the Earth's crust. The pie chart below shows you the abundance of these eight minerals.

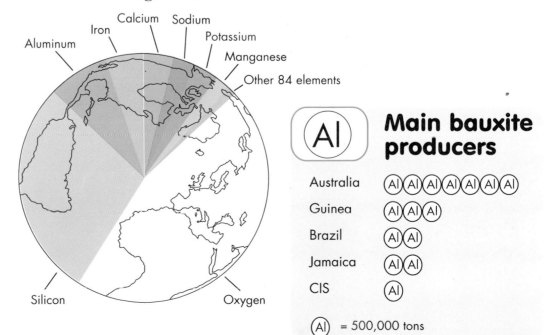

Crust: Thin layer of light rocks that vary in thickness. In the oceans it is an average of 3 miles in thickness. On the continents it is an average of 25 miles in thickness.

Mantle: About 1,800 miles thick. A hot, stiff, thick liquid rock called magma. Temperature of 1,472 – 4,532°F.

Aluminum   Iron   Calcium   Sodium   Potassium   Manganese   Other 84 elements

Silicon   Oxygen

(Al) Main bauxite producers

Australia	(Al)(Al)(Al)(Al)(Al)(Al)(Al)
Guinea	(Al)(Al)(Al)
Brazil	(Al)(Al)
Jamaica	(Al)(Al)
CIS	(Al)

(Al) = 500,000 tons

The area is rich in mined diamonds and metals. More than half of the world's diamonds come from Africa: gemstones from South Africa and industrial diamonds from central African countries — mainly Zaire.

Amazing – But True

★ The Cullinan, discovered in South Africa in 1905, was the largest uncut diamond. In its uncut state it was the size of a fist.

★ The rarest color of diamond is blood red. The largest is a 5.5-carat flawless stone found in South Africa in 1927.

★ Over 80% of the diamonds mined are used in industry and not for jewelry.

★ Gold miners need to dig out 2 tons of rock to find 1 ounce of gold.

Main diamond producers

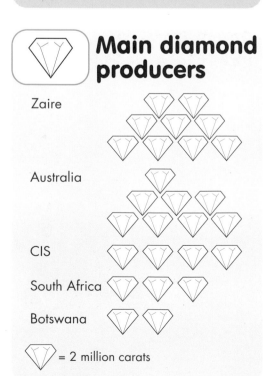

Zaire

Australia

CIS

South Africa

Botswana

⬦ = 2 million carats

Continental Drift

The crust of the Earth is broken up into pieces like a jigsaw puzzle. These pieces are called plates. The drifting of these plates means that the continents have not always been in the same place. This is called continental drift. It is thought that about 200 million years ago, at the beginning of the Jurassic period, there was one large continent called Pangea. This then split into two land masses. One was in the Northern Hemisphere and called Laurasia; the other was in the Southern Hemisphere and called Gondwanaland.

What the colors and symbols mean

Cenozoic   Intrusive rock   Upper Paleozoic

Lake Acer

Murphy Trench

Martin's Bay

120° W   110° W

Precambrian   Mesozoic   Lower Paleozoic

Symbol		Symbol	
▲	Volcano	⬦	Diamond
		Au	Gold
⊤	Coal	Fe	Iron
⬀	Natural gas	Pb	Lead
⬛	Oil	Ag	Silver
U	Uranium	Zn	Zinc
Cu	Copper	Sn	Tin
Mn	Manganese	Pt	Platinum

0   200   400   600 miles

1. The continents 175 million years ago in the Jurassic period

It is interesting to see how South America fitted into Africa.

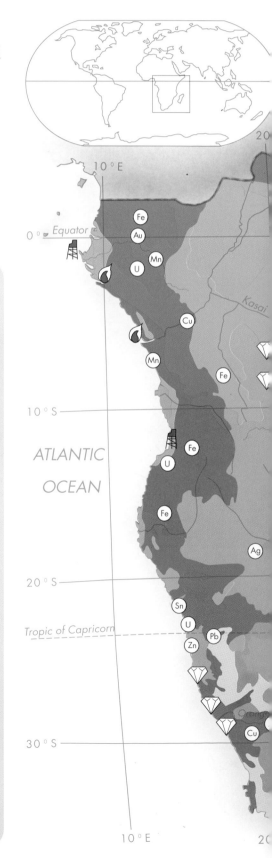

10° E

Equator 0°

Kasai

10° S

ATLANTIC OCEAN

Tropic of Capricorn

20° S

30° S

10° E

The continents 50 million years ago in the Tertiary period

3. The continents today

...y the Tertiary period the Atlantic, ...dian, and Pacific oceans existed. ...ou can also see that India had not ...ollided with Asia yet, and Australia ...as still attached to Antarctica.

The last map shows the continents as we know them today. But because they are still drifting apart the map will look different in 50 million years' time.

Did You Know

★ Scientists determined that the continents once fitted together like a jigsaw puzzle by studying and matching the fossils and rocks in different parts of the world.

★ The first known life on Earth began over 3 billion years ago. Fossils of tiny cells were found in a type of rock in South Africa, so small that hundreds would have fitted on the period at the end of this sentence.

★ The deepest mine in the world is the Western Deep Levels at Carletonville in South Africa. It is 12,391 feet deep.

Fossil Facts

★ The most famous living fossil is the coelacanth, a fish thought to be extinct until one was caught alive off the coast of South Africa in 1938.

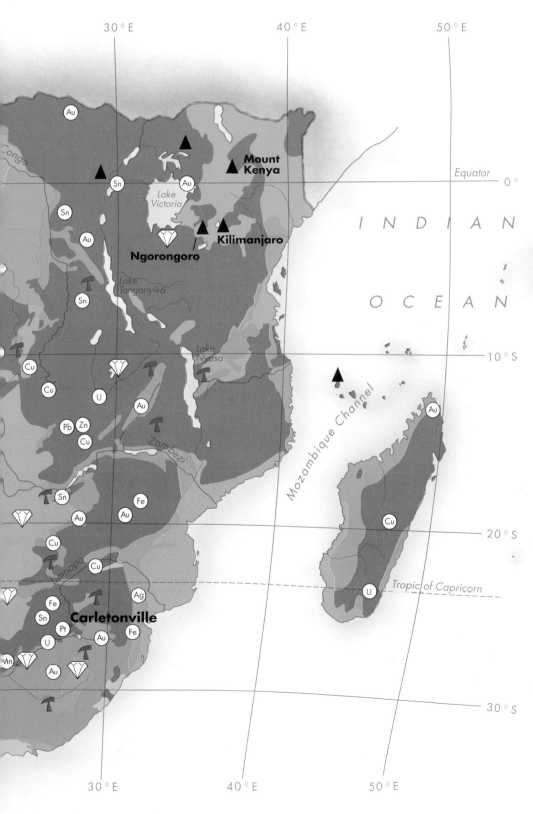

(Au) Main gold producers

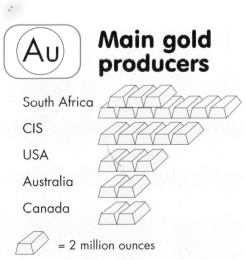

South Africa

CIS

USA

Australia

Canada

= 2 million ounces

America, Central

Most of Central America and the Caribbean is of relatively recent geological formation — generally comprising rock formations less than 100 million years old. This thin, winding section of land joins two much larger continents — North and South America.

? Did You Know

★ Radioactivity is used by geologists to work out the age of rocks. Many rocks contain uranium and potassium, which are radioactive as they slowly change into other elements. This process is so slow scientists can work out the age of the rocks.

★ At the end of the Tertiary period the last two major continents joined together. These were North and South America, and their joining separated the Atlantic Ocean from the Pacific Ocean. Central America created a land bridge for animals to move between the two large continents.

★ Silver is the most common precious metal, and it is lighter than gold. Almost half of the silver produced is used as a coating on photographic film.

★ On Trinidad is a lake that contains asphalt. Asphalt is the most viscous and heaviest form of oil.

★ San Salvador has been damaged, and on some occasions destroyed, by eathquakes nine times since the 16th century.

! Amazing – But True

★ Very rarely is the birth of a volcano seen, but in 1943, in Paricutín in Mexico, a farmer was working in a field when suddenly the ground started to shake. The following day there was a volcano where the field had been. Only a few volcanoes are born every century.

★ Pterygotus was a giant sea scorpion that lived 400 million years ago. It was a terrifying prehistoric sea animal more than 6 feet long.

Ag Main silver producers

Mexico Peru CIS USA Canada

= 5 million ounces

Geological Time Scale

The geological time scale covers the whole of the Earth's history from its origin 4.6 billion years ago to the present day. The largest divisions (eras) are subdivided into periods. The divisions are not equal lengths of time but are based on major evolutionary changes.

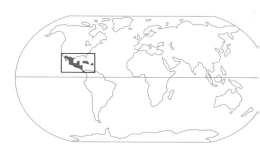

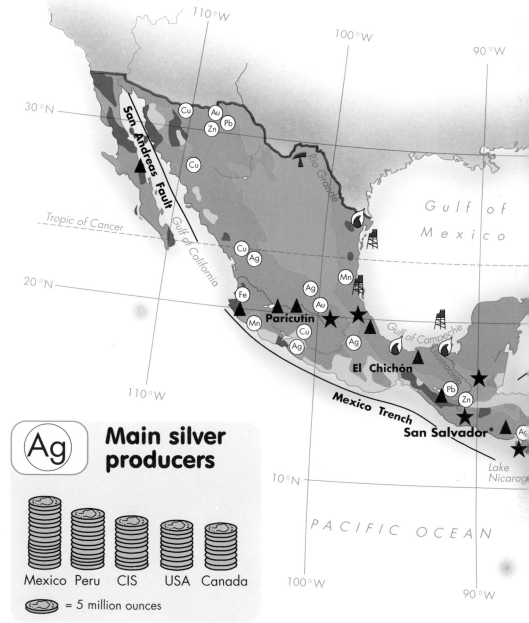

Era	Period	Meaning	Plant and animal life		Billions of yrs
CENOZOIC	QUATERNARY	The fourth formation.	Humans emerged.		2 – Today
	TERTIARY	The third formation.	Ape men appeared. Many mammals, birds, and flowering plants emerged.		65 – 2
MESOZOIC	CRETACEOUS	Chalky, as this is a common rock type in this period	Flowering plants appeared. Dinosaurs became extinct.		135 – 65
	JURASSIC	After the Jura Mountains in France.	Plant life was dominated by giant ferns. Ammonites were common. Dinosaurs ruled the land, and the first bird appeared.		180 – 135
	TRIASSIC	Rocks of this period in Germany were divided into 3 layers.	First dinosaurs and large sea reptiles appeared. Ammonites were common and there were luxuriant forests.		225 – 180
PALEOZOIC UPPER	PERMIAN	After the Perm district in the Russian Ural Mountains.	New reptiles and plants appeared on land. Ammonites swam in the sea, and trilobites died out.		270 – 225
	CARBONIFEROUS	Coal bearing.	Land was covered in swampy forests. First land animals and reptiles appeared.		350 – 270
LOWER	DEVONIAN	After Devon, a county in England.	Land plants became more common. Amphibians evolved.		395 – 350
	SILURIAN	After an ancient Welsh tribe.	First land plants appeared. Many fish and giant sea scorpions in the sea.		440 – 395
	ORDOVICIAN	After an ancient Welsh tribe.	The first fish appeared. Trilobites and graptolites were abundant.		500 – 440
	CAMBRIAN	After the Latin name for Wales, UK.	Jellyfish, sponges, coral, and trilobites abundant in the sea.		570 – 500
PRE-CAMBRIAN		Before the Cambrian.	Fossils are rare as the creatures were probably soft bodied like jellyfish. First simple creatures appeared 3.5 billion years ago.		4,600 – 570

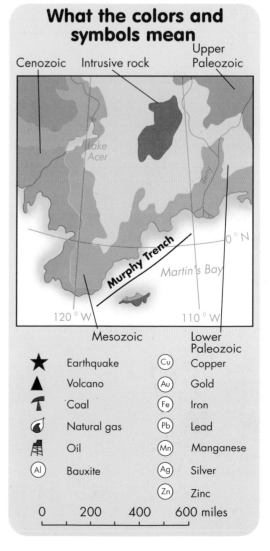

What the colors and symbols mean

Cenozoic Intrusive rock Upper Paleozoic

Lake Acer

Murphy Trench

Martin's Bay

Mesozoic Lower Paleozoic

★ Earthquake   (Cu) Copper
▲ Volcano   (Au) Gold
⊤ Coal   (Fe) Iron
◖ Natural gas (Pb) Lead
▤ Oil   (Mn) Manganese
(Al) Bauxite   (Ag) Silver
               (Zn) Zinc

0   200   400   600 miles

America, South

South America "broke away" from what is now Africa about 100 million years ago. Much of the land is igneous rock, formed from the cooling of molten minerals deep inside the earth. These rocks are hundreds of millions of years old.

Formation of Sedimentary Rocks

Sedimentary rocks make up only a small part of the Earth's crust, but they stretch over ¾ of the Earth's surface like a thin layer of skin. Sedimentary rocks are a layered rock made from bits of other rocks or shells. The particles are worn away from rocks on the land and washed into the sea by rivers. Here they settle on the sea bed. As more particles settle on top, the weight of these deposits causes the fragments at the bottom to be compressed together so hard that they become solid rock. The smaller particles washed into the sea as mud form a smooth, dark rock called shale. The larger sand grains form sandstone.

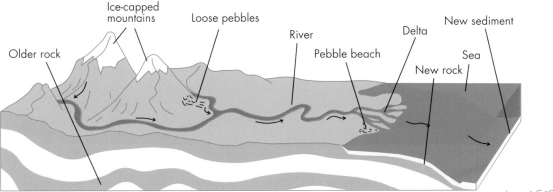

Types of Sedimentary Rock

Chalk
A soft, white rock made of very fine grains. Makes a white mark if you rub it on something hard.

Limestone
A gray, white, or yellow rock. Sometimes very hard, and you may be able to see layers in it.

Sandstone
A rock made from grains of sand. You can often see layers. It feels rough and the sand may even rub off it.

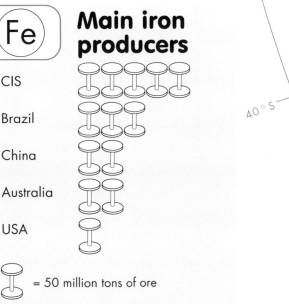

Fe **Main iron producers**

CIS

Brazil

China

Australia

USA

= 50 million tons of ore

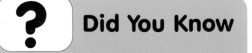

? Did You Know

★ The eruptian of Ruiz in Colombia melted huge quantities of snow, which mixed with the soil to make an enormous tidal wave of mud.

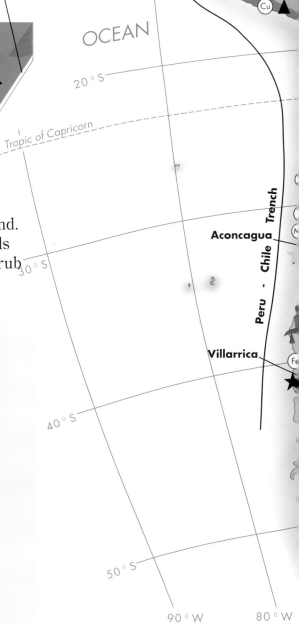

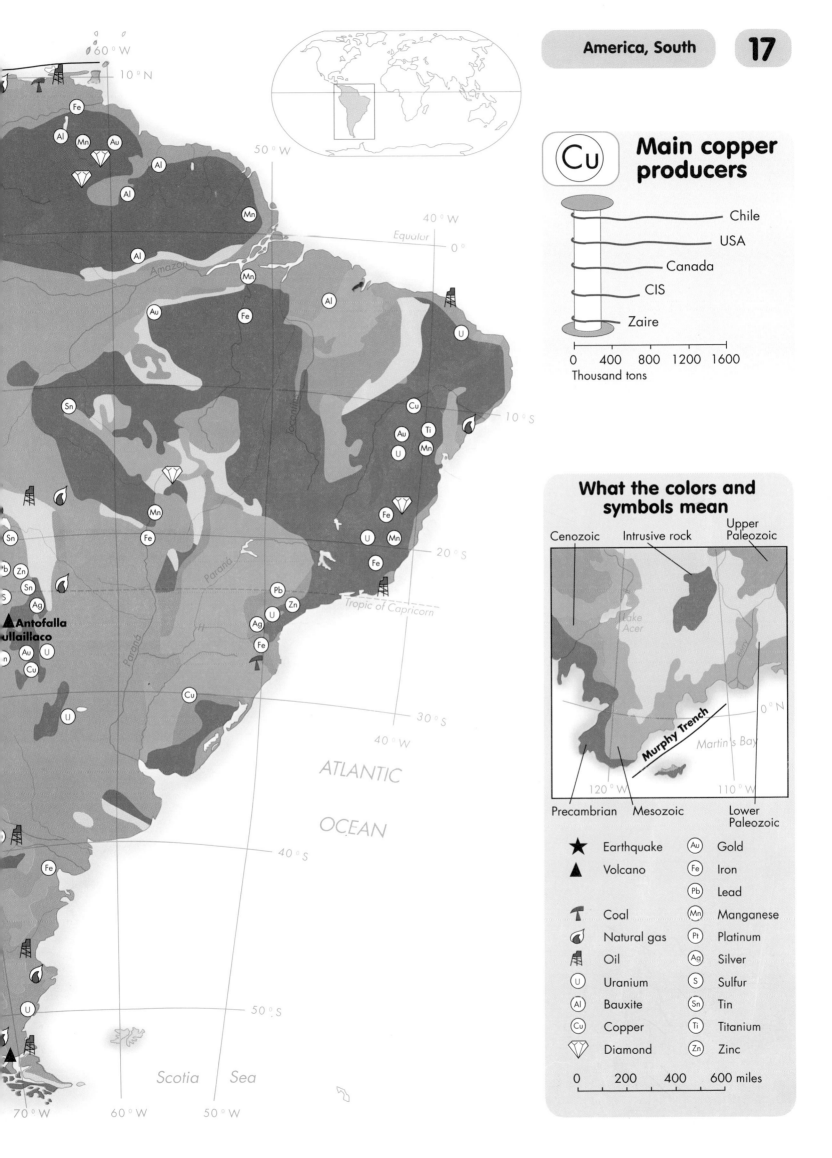

Cu **Main copper producers**

Chile
USA
Canada
CIS
Zaire

| 0 | 400 | 800 | 1200 | 1600 |
Thousand tons

What the colors and symbols mean

Cenozoic   Intrusive rock   Upper Paleozoic

Lake Acer

Murphy Trench   Martin's Bay

0° N

120° W   110° W

Precambrian   Mesozoic   Lower Paleozoic

★	Earthquake	Au	Gold
▲	Volcano	Fe	Iron
		Pb	Lead
⊺	Coal	Mn	Manganese
◖	Natural gas	Pt	Platinum
⚒	Oil	Ag	Silver
U	Uranium	S	Sulfur
Al	Bauxite	Sn	Tin
Cu	Copper	Ti	Titanium
◆	Diamond	Zn	Zinc

| 0 | 200 | 400 | 600 miles |

Map labels

60° W
10° N
Fe
Al Mn Au
Al
Al
Mn
50° W
Al
40° W
Equator
0°
Al
Amazon
Mn
Au Fe
Al
U
Sn
Cu
Au Ti
U Mn
10° S
Mn
Fe
Fe
U Mn
20° S
Fe
Parana
Pb
U Zn
Tropic of Capricorn
Sn
Zn
Sn
Ag
Ag
Fe
Antofalla
ullaillaco
Au U
Cu
Fe
U
Cu
Parana
30° S
40° W
ATLANTIC
OCEAN
40° S
Fe
50° S
Scotia Sea
70° W   60° W   50° W

Antarctica differs from the north polar region because underneath the permanent ice cover lies a rocky continent, not simply a frozen ice cap. It has remained largely unexplored by humans — until quite recently. Several nations have established claims to Antarctic territories, hoping eventually to mine some of the considerable untapped natural resources of the continent.

Most fossils are found in areas that were once in or near the sea where sedimentary rocks are formed. Fossils are easily found and collected when they have been exposed by water and wind wearing away the surrounding rock. On this page are some examples of fossils you can collect.

Ammonite

Ammonite fossils are found in marine rocks formed during the Triassic and Cretaceous periods. Their curly and patterned shells fossilized so well that you can see the detail on the fossils.

Brachiopod

Underneath   Side

Brachiopods are found in limestones, mudstones, and shales dating from the Cambrian to the Carboniferous periods. They can also be found alive on the sea bed today. They are "living" fossils.

Echinoid

Echinoids are round or heart-shaped and are found in rocks of the Jurassic period. But the spines are rarely preserved as fossils. Today's sea urchins can be found with their spiny covering.

Fish

Fish were the first animals to have backbones. These fossils are hard to find, but the hard teeth of sharks can be found in rocks from the Cretaceous and Tertiary periods.

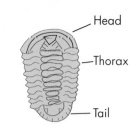

Trilobite

Head

Thorax

Tail

Trilobites had a head, a body called the thorax, and a tail. The thorax was segmented so that some trilobites could roll up into a ball. They can be found in rocks from the Cambrian to the Carboniferous periods.

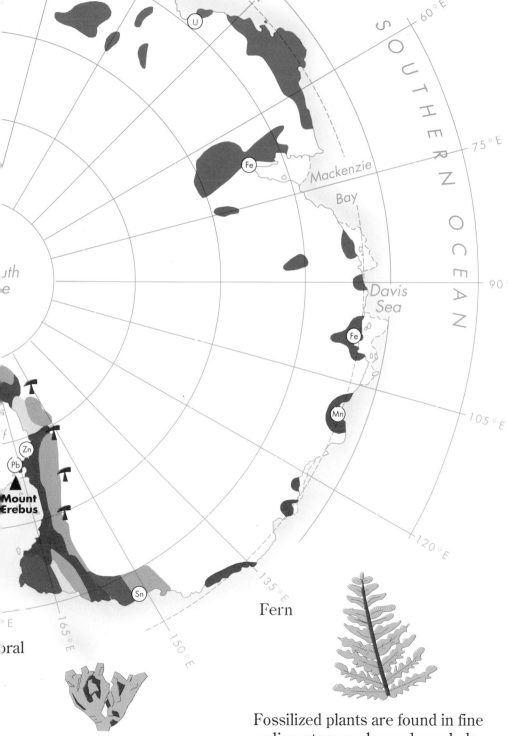

SOUTHERN OCEAN

Mackenzie Bay

Davis Sea

Mount Erebus

ral

ith e

uth e

Fern

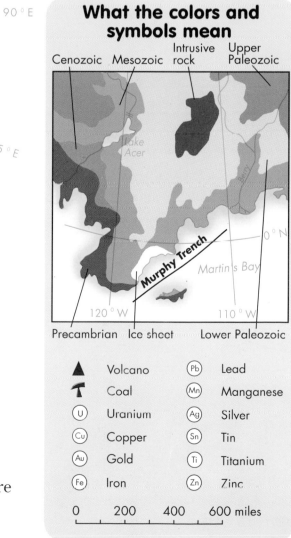

Fossilized plants are found in fine sedimentary rocks such as shale. Many of the prehistoric plants were giant treelike ferns. These were common 300 million years ago.

ral fossils may be found as single als or as a group. They are ally found in limestone.

Amazing – But True

★ Antarctica had a tropical climate millions of years ago.

★ Mammoths have been buried in ice, making fossils that looked exactly as they did when they were alive. As these mammoths have been kept in a natural deep freeze for thousands of years, some people have tried to eat the steaks cut from them.

What the colors and symbols mean

Cenozoic Mesozoic Intrusive rock Upper Paleozoic

Lake Acer

Murphy Trench

Martin's Bay

120°W 110°W

Precambrian Ice sheet Lower Paleozoic

▲ Volcano   Pb Lead
⊤ Coal   Mn Manganese
U Uranium   Ag Silver
Cu Copper   Sn Tin
Au Gold   Ti Titanium
Fe Iron   Zn Zinc

0   200   400   600 miles

Asia is the largest continent, with several others "bolted on" to it — Europe, Africa, and the Indian subcontinent. East Asia is a mixture of ancient Precambrian rock and new formations that date from all the geological periods.

Formation of Coal

Most of the coal in the world is derived from plants that grew in the Carboniferous period of the Earth's history, when whole regions of the Earth were covered with swamps filled with gigantic ferns and trees.

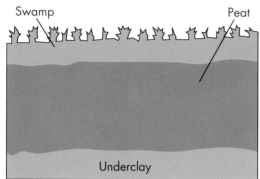

The plants died and fell into the swamps, which then decayed and were covered with mud and clay. More plants died, decayed, and were covered with mud and clay. These built up in layers sandwiched between mud and clay.

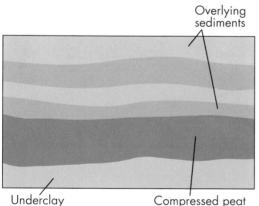

The Earth's crust enfolded these sediments, and then heat and pressure changed them into rock, forcing the water from the decayed matter. The original plants have now been changed into coal.

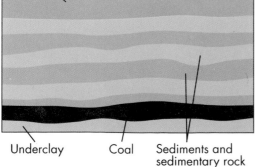

! Amazing – But True

★ Tokyo's architects and planners prepared for the future by designing buildings with supporting struts that resist earthquakes. These were tested in December 1987, when an earthquake registered 6.6 on the Richter scale. The skyscrapers swayed, but they all stayed in one piece.

★ The scientists that study volcanoes are called vulcanologists. They are very brave and often explore the inside of craters. In 1934 two men went 1,365 feet down inside a live volcano in Japan.

Main coal producers

Million Tons

 Did You Know

★ China has the worst record for earthquake deaths. An earthquake in 1556 killed 830,000 people, and in 1976 an earthquake killed 750,000 people. The 1976 quake registered 8.2 on the Richter scale.

★ It is in coal mining that the greatest advances in mining methods have taken place.

What the colors and symbols mean

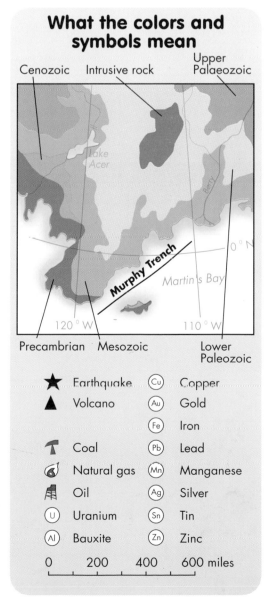

Cenozoic   Intrusive rock   Upper Palaeozoic

Precambrian   Mesozoic   Lower Paleozoic

★	Earthquake	Cu	Copper
▲	Volcano	Au	Gold
		Fe	Iron
⛏	Coal	Pb	Lead
⛽	Natural gas	Mn	Manganese
🛢	Oil	Ag	Silver
U	Uranium	Sn	Tin
Al	Bauxite	Zn	Zinc

0   200   400   600 miles

Fossil Facts

★ In the Gobi Desert in Mongolia, fossils of two dinosaurs locked in combat were found. They had died still clinging to each other.

★ The only survivor of a group of plants that flourished 200 million years ago is the ginkgo, a type of tree native to China and Japan.

 Main sulfur producers

USA	Ⓢ Ⓢ Ⓢ Ⓢ Ⓢ Ⓢ Ⓢ Ⓢ Ⓢ Ⓢ Ⓢ
Canada	Ⓢ Ⓢ Ⓢ Ⓢ Ⓢ Ⓢ Ⓢ
Japan	Ⓢ Ⓢ
Mexico	Ⓢ Ⓢ
Germany	Ⓢ Ⓢ

Ⓢ = 1,000 tons

Asia, Southeast

The long peninsula and scattered land masses of Southeast Asia are almost all of recent mountainous rock formation. Earthquakes and volcanic eruptions are frequent.

? Did You Know

★ A crater at the top of a volcano that is more than a mile across is called a caldera.

★ The ash that falls from volcanoes is very rich in minerals. The most fertile soils of all are found in hot, damp climates at the foot of volcanoes.

★ After Indonesia's Krakatoa erupted in 1883, vivid colors of red, purple, and pink were seen at sunset all over the world. This was due to the tiny particles of dust carried in the air, disrupting the path of the sunlight.

! Amazing – But True

★ There are a million earthquakes a year, and a large earthquake happens almost every two weeks. These are usually in the sea, so little damage is caused.

★ The world's largest caldera is that of Toba in Sumatra, Indonesia. The caldera covers an area of 685 square miles.

★ The world's most valuable gemstone is a ruby found in Burma. This cut stone weighs 1,184 carats.

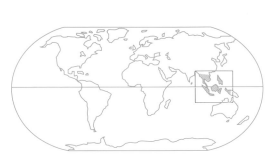

What is an Earthquake ?

Earthquakes often happen along the edges of the plates that make up the Earth's crust. These plates are always moving and sliding past each other very slowly. Occasionally one plate gets stuck against another plate, which results in a series of violent jerks until the plates suddenly slip past each other. This is an earthquake. If you drop a pebble in a pond, the waves spread out from the center. The vibrations of an earthquake travel out from the center in the same way. The center of the earthquake is called the focus, and the point on the ground directly above it is called the epicenter.

Measuring Earthquakes

The power and magnitude of an earthquake is measured on the Richter scale. This was developed by C.F. Richter in 1935 to compare the sizes of earthquakes in California. The scale runs from 0 to 9 and each number is 10 times more powerful than the number below it. The higher the number on the scale, the larger the earthquake. The strongest earthquake so far recorded had a Richter scale value of 9.

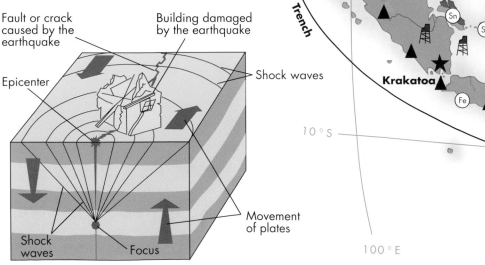

Fault or crack caused by the earthquake

Building damaged by the earthquake

Epicenter

Shock waves

Shock waves

Focus

Movement of plates

Sn Main tin producers

Brazil
China
Malaysia
Indonesia
Bolivia

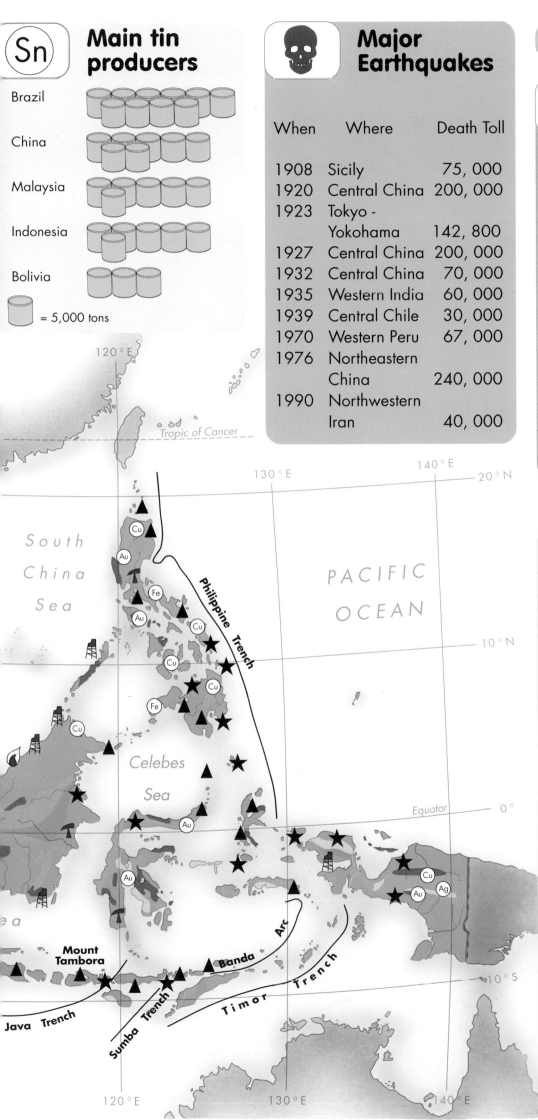

= 5,000 tons

Major Earthquakes

When	Where	Death Toll
1908	Sicily	75, 000
1920	Central China	200, 000
1923	Tokyo - Yokohama	142, 800
1927	Central China	200, 000
1932	Central China	70, 000
1935	Western India	60, 000
1939	Central Chile	30, 000
1970	Western Peru	67, 000
1976	Northeastern China	240, 000
1990	Northwestern Iran	40, 000

Fossil Facts

★ The largest fossil insect ever found lived in the Carboniferous period. It was a giant dragonfly called meganeura with a wingspan of 2 feet 6 inches. These ruled the air from 300 to 195 million years ago, until the flying reptiles joined them.

★ The stegosaurus was the dinosaur with the smallest brain in comparison to its body size. Its brain was the size of a large walnut, but its body weighed nearly 2 tons.

What the colors and symbols mean

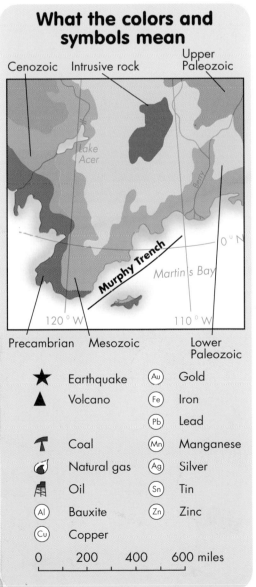

Cenozoic Intrusive rock Upper Paleozoic
Precambrian Mesozoic Lower Paleozoic

★ Earthquake   Au Gold
▲ Volcano   Fe Iron
                Pb Lead
⛏ Coal   Mn Manganese
Natural gas   Ag Silver
Oil   Sn Tin
Al Bauxite   Zn Zinc
Cu Copper

0   200   400   600 miles

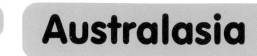

Australasia is dominated by the huge land mass of Australia, an old Precambrian continent, worn down and flattened by millions of years of erosion. The surrounding islands are young and volcanically active.

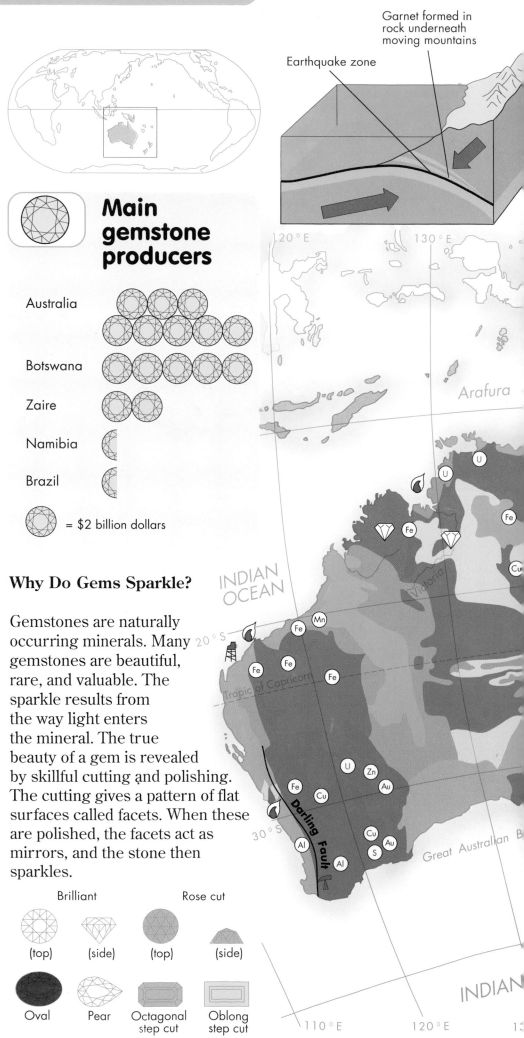

Garnet formed in rock underneath moving mountains

Earthquake zone

? Did You Know

★ Sapphires and rubies are both varieties of corundum. Their different colors result from chemical impurities.

Main gemstone producers

Australia	◉◉◉◉◉◉◉◉◉◉
Botswana	◉◉◉◉◉
Zaire	◉◉
Namibia	◖
Brazil	◖

◉ = $2 billion dollars

Why Do Gems Sparkle?

Gemstones are naturally occurring minerals. Many gemstones are beautiful, rare, and valuable. The sparkle results from the way light enters the mineral. The true beauty of a gem is revealed by skillful cutting and polishing. The cutting gives a pattern of flat surfaces called facets. When these are polished, the facets act as mirrors, and the stone then sparkles.

Brilliant   Rose cut

(top)   (side)   (top)   (side)

Oval   Pear   Octagonal step cut   Oblong step cut

What the colors and symbols mean

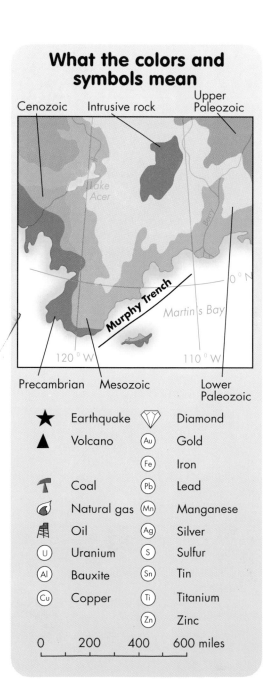

Cenozoic   Intrusive rock   Upper Paleozoic

Lake Acer

Murphy Trench

Martin's Bay

120° W   110° W   0° N

Precambrian   Mesozoic   Lower Paleozoic

★	Earthquake	◇	Diamond	
▲	Volcano	Au	Gold	
		Fe	Iron	
⊤	Coal	Pb	Lead	
⌀	Natural gas	Mn	Manganese	
⌸	Oil	Ag	Silver	
U	Uranium	S	Sulfur	
Al	Bauxite	Sn	Tin	
Cu	Copper	Ti	Titanium	
		Zn	Zinc	

0   200   400   600 miles

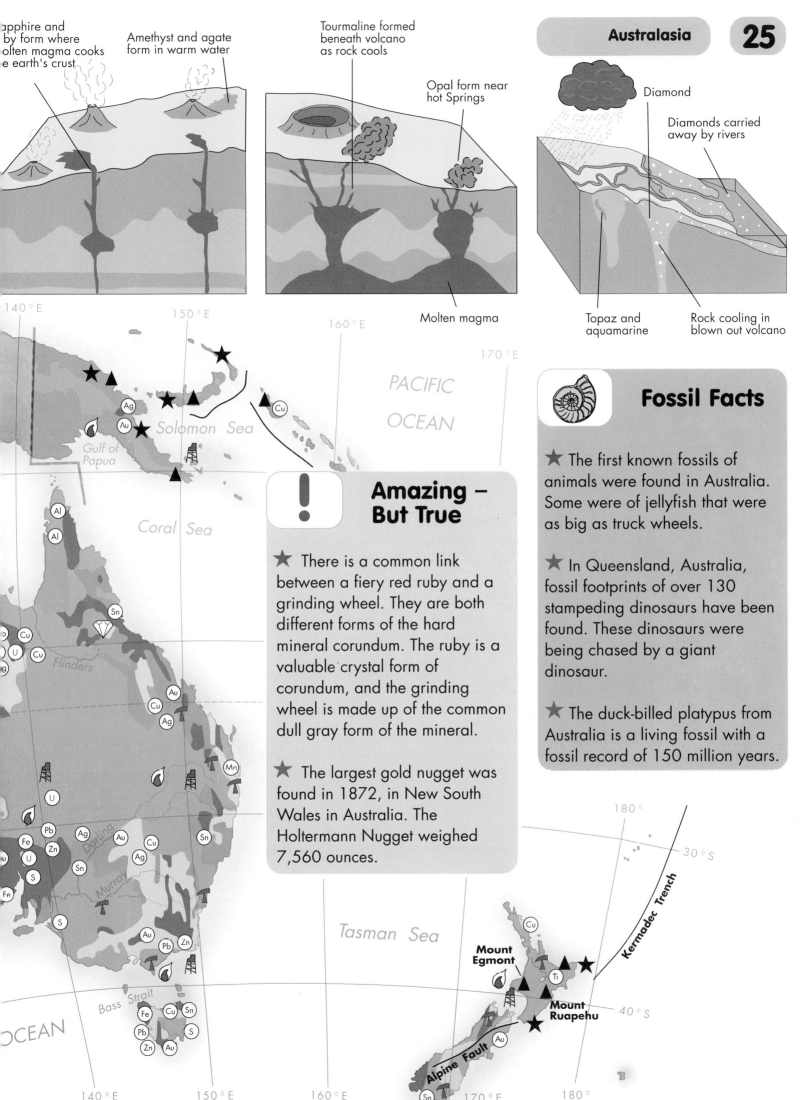

apphire and
by form where
olten magma cooks
e earth's crust

Amethyst and agate
form in warm water

Tourmaline formed
beneath volcano
as rock cools

Opal form near
hot Springs

Diamond

Diamonds carried
away by rivers

Molten magma

Topaz and
aquamarine

Rock cooling in
blown out volcano

140°E

150°E

160°E

170°E

PACIFIC

OCEAN

Ag

Au

Cu

Solomon Sea

Gulf of
Papua

Al

Al

Coral Sea

Sn

Cu

U

Cu

Flinders

Au

Cu

Ag

Mn

U

Pb

Ag

Au

Cu

Sn

Fe

Zn

U

Ag

S

Sn

Fe

S

Darling

Murray

Au

Pb

Zn

Fe

Cu

Sn

Pb

Zn

Au

S

Bass Strait

OCEAN

140°E

150°E

Amazing – But True

⭐ There is a common link between a fiery red ruby and a grinding wheel. They are both different forms of the hard mineral corundum. The ruby is a valuable crystal form of corundum, and the grinding wheel is made up of the common dull gray form of the mineral.

⭐ The largest gold nugget was found in 1872, in New South Wales in Australia. The Holtermann Nugget weighed 7,560 ounces.

Fossil Facts

⭐ The first known fossils of animals were found in Australia. Some were of jellyfish that were as big as truck wheels.

⭐ In Queensland, Australia, fossil footprints of over 130 stampeding dinosaurs have been found. These dinosaurs were being chased by a giant dinosaur.

⭐ The duck-billed platypus from Australia is a living fossil with a fossil record of 150 million years.

180°

30°S

Kermadec Trench

Tasman Sea

Cu

Mount
Egmont

Ti

40°S

Mount
Ruapehu

Au

Alpine Fault

Sn

160°E

170°E

180°

Canada occupies the largest part of the North American continent and is rich in minerals and metals. The geological structure is very ancient in the east and gets progressively younger to the west.

Main uranium producers

Canada	Ⓤ Ⓤ Ⓤ Ⓤ Ⓤ Ⓤ Ⓤ Ⓤ
USA	Ⓤ Ⓤ Ⓤ
South Africa	Ⓤ Ⓤ Ⓤ
Namibia	Ⓤ Ⓤ
Niger	Ⓤ Ⓤ

Ⓤ = 1,500 tons

History of the Earth in a Year

January
1st   Earth's history began.
February
March
22nd   First simple creatures appeared.
April
May
June
July
August
September
October
November
15th   Trilobites were abundant.
20th   First fish appeared.
25th   Giant sea scorpions were in the sea.
        First land plants appeared.
December
3rd   Coal was being formed.
13th   First Dinosaurs appeared.
16th   First bird appeared.
20th   First flowering plants appeared.
        Dinosaurs became extinct.
31st   At 8.20 P.M. humans appeared.

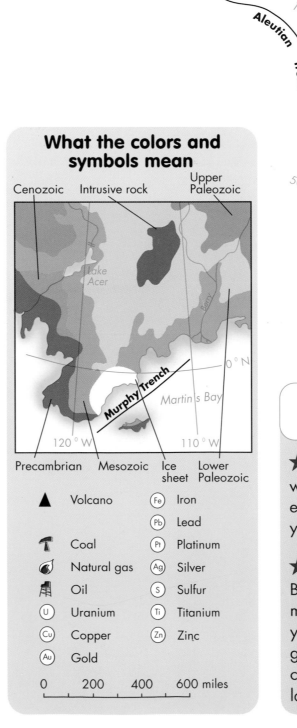

What the colors and symbols mean

Cenozoic   Intrusive rock   Upper Paleozoic

Precambrian   Mesozoic   Ice sheet   Lower Paleozoic

▲	Volcano	Ⓕⓔ	Iron
		Ⓟⓑ	Lead
⛏	Coal	Ⓟⓣ	Platinum
⬤	Natural gas	Ⓐⓖ	Silver
⛏	Oil	Ⓢ	Sulfur
Ⓤ	Uranium	Ⓣⓘ	Titanium
Ⓒⓤ	Copper	Ⓩⓝ	Zinc
Ⓐⓤ	Gold		

0   200   400   600 miles

? Did You Know

★ The oldest known rocks are in western Greenland and are estimated to be 3.57 billion years old.

★ The rocks around Hudson Bay are the roots of an ancient mountain range. Over a billion years of erosion by rivers, glaciers, and wind has completely flattened the landscape.

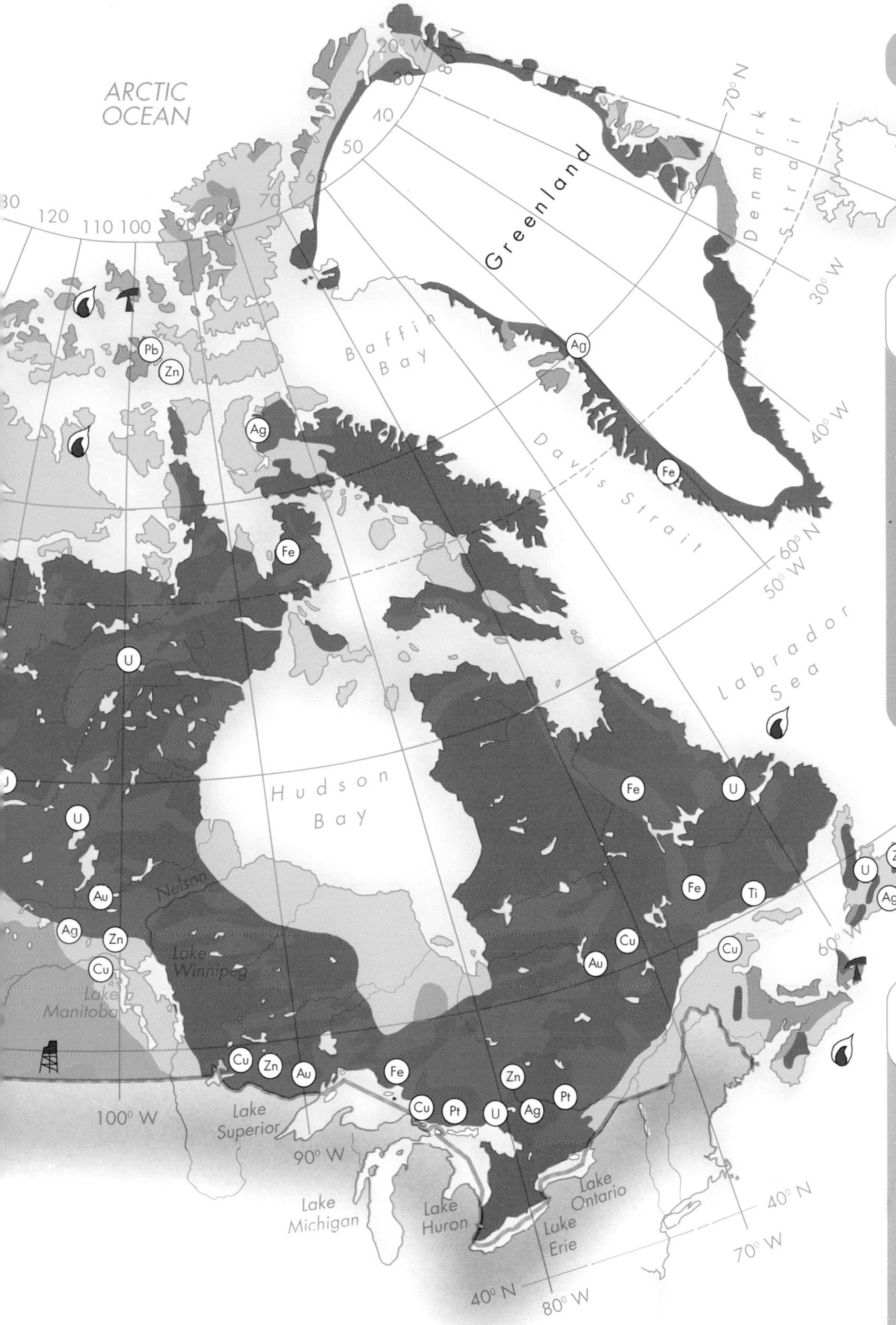

The map shows markers: ARCTIC OCEAN, 20° W, 80° N, 10, 50, 60, 70° N, 20° W, 30° W, Denmark Strait, Greenland, 30, 120, 110 100, 90, 80, 70, Baffin Bay, Davis Strait, Fe, Ag, 40° W, 50° W, Labrador Sea, 60° N, ATLANTIC OCEAN, 50° N.

Map mineral markers: Pb, Zn, U, U, U, Au, Ag, Zn, Cu, Lake Winnipeg, Lake Manitoba, Nelson, Hudson Bay, Fe, U, Fe, Ti, U, Zn, Fe, Ag, Cu, Au, Cu, Cu, Zn, Au, Fe, Zn, Pt, Cu, Pt, U, Ag, Pt, Lake Superior, Lake Michigan, Lake Huron, Lake Erie, Lake Ontario, 100° W, 90° W, 80° W, 70° W, 40° N, 40° N.

Fossil Facts

★ Fossils of insects are rare because their bodies are very delicate. Some prehistoric insects have been found preserved in amber. The insects were trapped in the sticky liquid called resin, which leaked from pine trees. This hardened to form a clear yellow stone called amber.

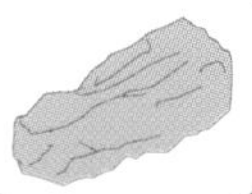

Hardness of rock

Each mineral has a certain hardness. This can be tested by scratching one mineral against another. The harder mineral scratches the softer one. In 1822 a German called Friedrich Mohs invented the Mohs hardness scale. Ten minerals numbered 1 to 10 make up this scale, so that the hardness of other minerals can be found if they are scratched by a mineral in the Mohs scale. The softest is talc, 1, and the hardest is diamond, 10.

You can test for hardness using

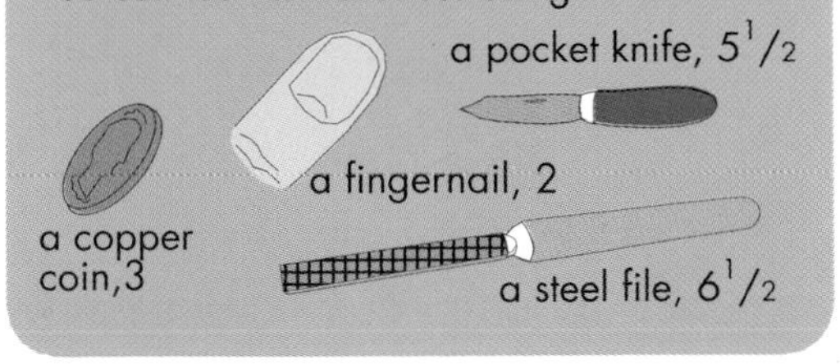

a pocket knife, $5\frac{1}{2}$

a fingernail, 2

a copper coin, 3

a steel file, $6\frac{1}{2}$

Amazing – But True

★ One ton of uranium can produce as much energy as 20,000 tons of coal.

★ The first horses were the size of cats and lived in the forests of North America 55 million years ago.

(Zn) Main zinc producers

Canada	Zn Zn Zn Zn Zn Zn Zn Zn Zn Zn Zn Zn
CIS	Zn Zn Zn Zn Zn Zn Zn Zn Zn
Australia	Zn Zn Zn Zn Zn Zn Zn Zn
China	Zn Zn Zn Zn Zn Zn
Peru	Zn Zn Zn Zn Zn Zn

(Zn) = 100,000 tons

The former USSR stretches from eastern Europe across the vast Precambrian plains of northern Asia until it reaches the newer Mesozoic rock formations of the Far East. The central Urals area is heavily mined for iron, copper, zinc, and bauxite.

? Did You Know

★ The United States has the greatest underground pipeline system in the world. It carries oil and natural gas the length and breadth of the country. There are also long oil and natural gas pipelines in the CIS and the Middle East.

What the colors and symbols mean

Cenozoic   Intrusive rock   Upper Paleozoic

Precambrian   Mesozoic   Lower Paleozoic

★ Earthquake	(Au) Gold		
▲ Volcano	(Fe) Iron		
	(Pb) Lead		
⊤ Coal	(Mn) Manganese		
🝁 Natural gas	(Ag) Silver		
🛢 Oil	(S) Sulfur		
(U) Uranium	(Sn) Tin		
(Al) Bauxite	(Ti) Titanium		
(Cu) Copper	(Zn) Zinc		
◇ Diamond			

0   200   400   600 miles

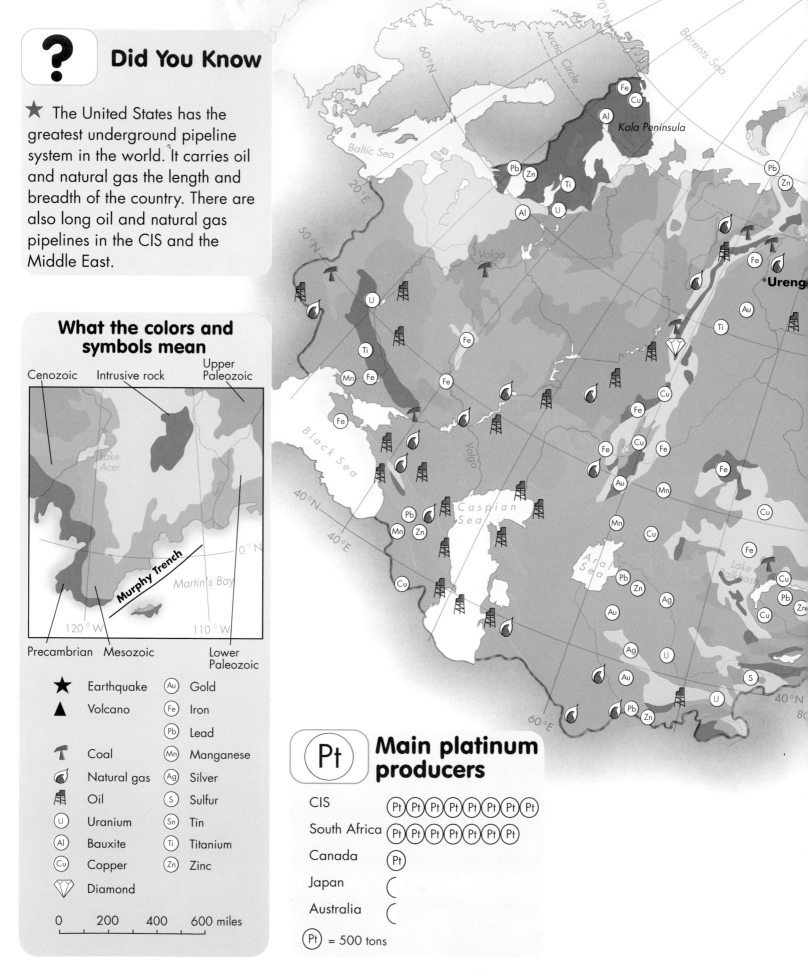

(Pt) Main platinum producers

CIS	(Pt)(Pt)(Pt)(Pt)(Pt)(Pt)(Pt)(Pt)
South Africa	(Pt)(Pt)(Pt)(Pt)(Pt)(Pt)(Pt)
Canada	(Pt)
Japan	(
Australia	(

(Pt) = 500 tons

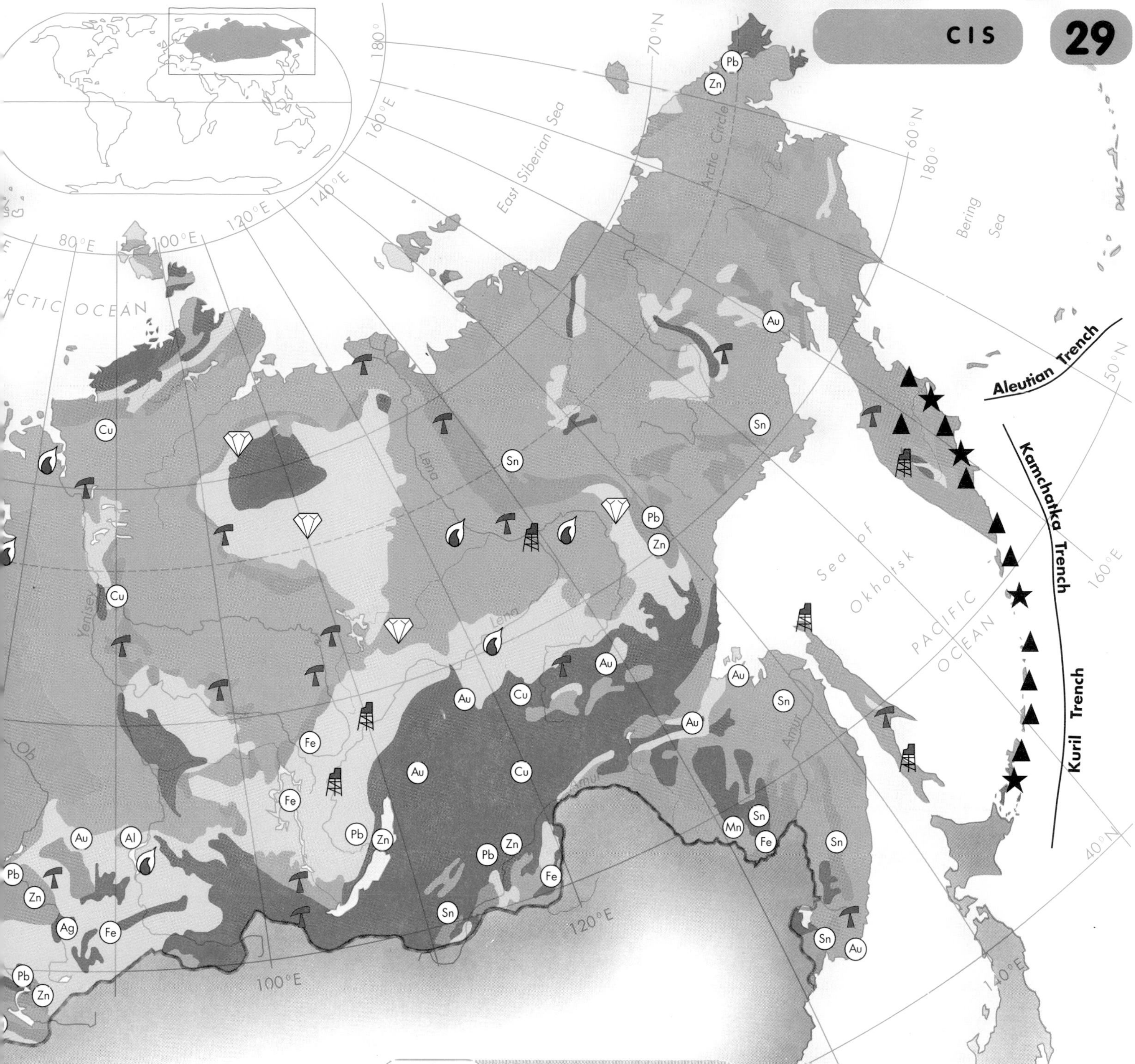

CTIC OCEAN
East Siberian Sea
Arctic Circle
Bering Sea
Sea of Okhotsk
PACIFIC OCEAN
Aleutian Trench
Kamchatka Trench
Kuril Trench
Lena
Yenisey
Ob
Amur
70°N
60°N
50°N
40°N
80°E
100°E
120°E
140°E
160°E
180°
Cu
Au
Sn
Pb
Zn
Fe
Al
Ag
Mn

! Amazing – But True

★ The deepest penetration into the Earth's crust is an exploratory well drilled on the Kola Peninsula, CIS. In 1990 it was 3,695 feet deep.

★ Platinum is the most expensive metal in the world, and one of its special qualities is that it does not tarnish.

★ The largest gas deposit in the world is at Urengoy in the CIS.

Mn Main manganese producers

CIS	Mn Mn Mn Mn Mn Mn Mn Mn Mn Mn
South Africa	Mn Mn Mn Mn
Brazil	Mn Mn Mn
Gabon	Mn Mn Mn
Australia	Mn Mn

Mn = 1,000 tons

Fossil Facts

★ The largest prehistoric fish was carcharodon megalodon, which lived over 20 million years ago. Its teeth were the size of an adult's hand, and four people could have stood in its open mouth.

Europe is the most heavily exploited continent for its natural resources. Since humans started mining on a large scale in Roman times, Europe has been a leading producer of iron and coal.

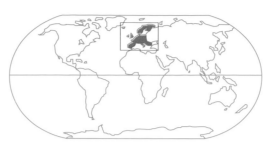

! Amazing – But True

★ There are more than 600 active volcanoes on earth, and almost a third of these are on Iceland.

★ Other planets also have volcanoes. On Mars there is a volcano called Mount Olympus.

★ Pumice is a rock light enough to float on water. It is formed from a type of lava.

★ The purest, crystal-clear form of calcite is called Iceland spar. This can literally make you see double. If you place a piece of Iceland spar over a line of type in this book, you will see two lines when you look through the crystal.

Fossil Facts

★ In Europe 22 million years ago lived the tanystropheus. This reptile had a neck 13 feet long, which was twice the length of its body.

★ The oldest known flowering plant is a tiny bloom discovered in Sweden, where it was preserved in mud from the Cretaceous period.

Evolution of Mankind

Through the evidence of fossilized skeletons we know how humans evolved. Below are five examples of human development.

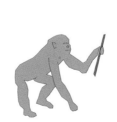

Ramapithecus

"early manlike ape"
15 million years ago

Australopithecus

"earliest ape-man"
4 million years ago

Homo erectus

"upright ape-man"
1 million years ago

Homo sapien Neanderthal m

"intelligent man"
100,000 years ag

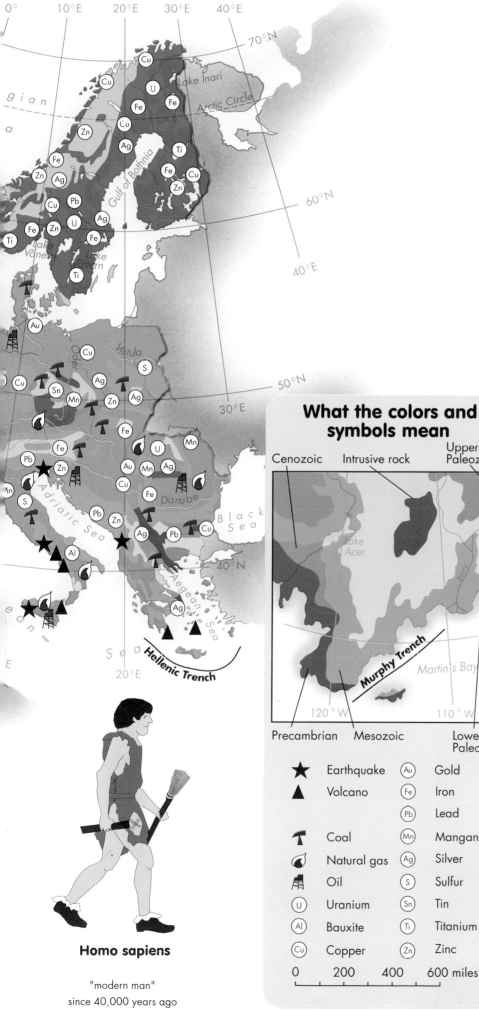

What is a Volcano ?

Volcanoes form along the edges of the crust plates. When magma escapes from inside the Earth it becomes lava. If lava is thick and sticky it forms a mountain shaped like a cone, and a volcano is born. Sometimes lava is very liquid and can flow a long way.

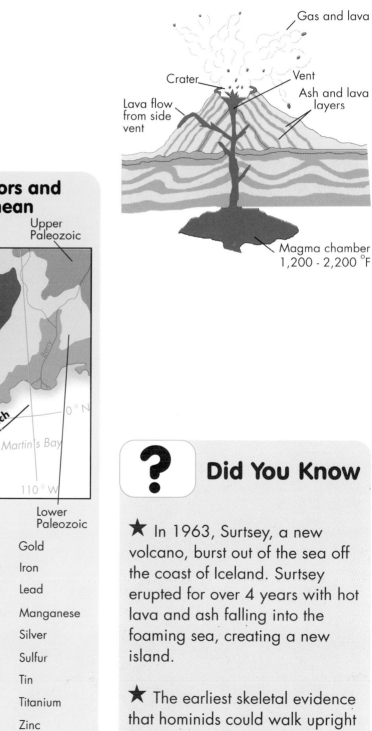

- Gas and lava
- Crater
- Vent
- Ash and lava layers
- Lava flow from side vent
- Magma chamber 1,200 - 2,200 °F

What the colors and symbols mean

Cenozoic Intrusive rock Upper Paleozoic

Lake Acer

Murphy Trench

Martin's Bay

Precambrian Mesozoic Lower Paleozoic

★	Earthquake	Au	Gold
▲	Volcano	Fe	Iron
		Pb	Lead
⛏	Coal	Mn	Manganese
🌢	Natural gas	Ag	Silver
⛽	Oil	S	Sulfur
U	Uranium	Sn	Tin
Al	Bauxite	Ti	Titanium
Cu	Copper	Zn	Zinc

0   200   400   600 miles

Homo sapiens

"modern man" since 40,000 years ago

? Did You Know

★ In 1963, Surtsey, a new volcano, burst out of the sea off the coast of Iceland. Surtsey erupted for over 4 years with hot lava and ash falling into the foaming sea, creating a new island.

★ The earliest skeletal evidence that hominids could walk upright on two feet was a female skeleton named "Lucy."

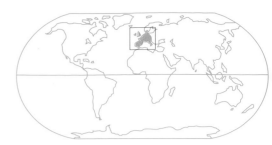

Heavily industrialized and populated, Western Europe is a source for many raw and refined natural products. It is responsible for about one third of the world's Gross Domestic Product.

Formation of Fossils

Fossils are the hardened remains or impressions of plants and animals that lived a long time ago. In these diagrams you can see how fossils are made.

Dead ammonites sink to ocean floor

The ammonite's swam in the sea until they died, and their bodies sank to the sea bed. Their bodies decayed and disappeared, but their hard shells became buried in the mud and sand. Layers of mud and sand settled on top of the shells over thousands of years and compressed the layers beneath them so hard that they became solid rock.

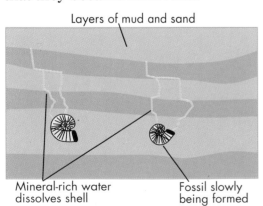

Layers of mud and sand

Mineral-rich water dissolves shell

Fossil slowly being formed

Water seeps through the rock and dissolves the original shells, leaving minerals in their place that form exactly the same shape. The fossils are only exposed when the Earth's crust pushes up the sea bed to form land and the rocks are worn away by water and wind.

Fossil Facts

★ Early in the Cambrian period animals started to develop hard parts such as shells and chalky external skeletons. As these fossilized easily, we know more about the animal life from the Cambrian times onward.

★ The largest dinosaur egg ever found was discovered in France. It was as large as a football and was laid by a sauropod.

★ The smallest known adult dinosaur was only 2 feet long. It was found in Scotland and called saltopus.

★ The fossil record shows that there have been about six mass extinctions over the past 500 million years. The extinction of the dinosaurs was only one of them. It occurred quickly, lasting only a few thousand years.

The study of fossils is called paleontology.

Trace fossils are the things that animals leave behind like burrows, tracks, or footprints.

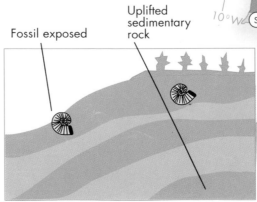

Fossil exposed

Uplifted sedimentary rock

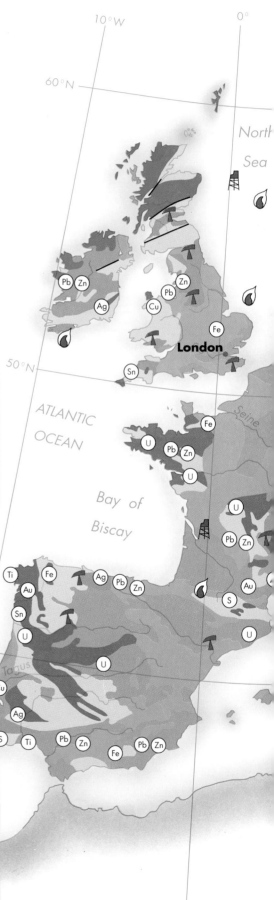

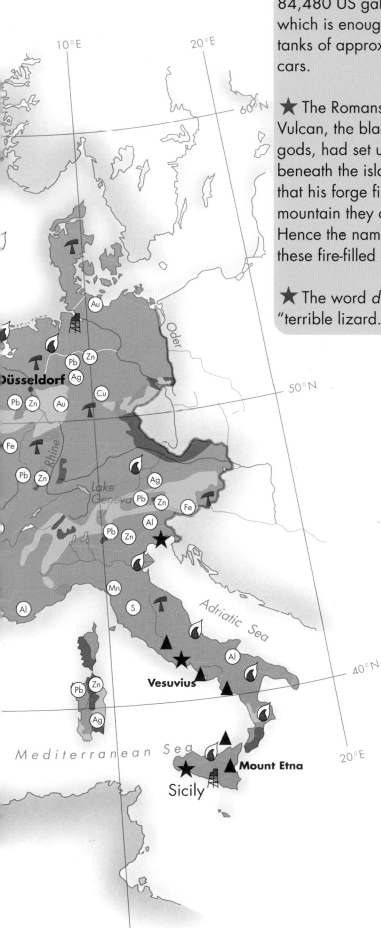

! Amazing – But True

★ At least 20% of the world's oil comes from beneath the sea. One North Sea oil rig can produce 84,480 US gallons of oil a day, which is enough to fill the gas tanks of approximately 5,000 cars.

★ The Romans thought that Vulcan, the blacksmith of the gods, had set up his forge beneath the island of Sicily and that his forge fire burned inside a mountain they called Vulcano. Hence the name of volcano for these fire-filled mountains.

★ The word *dinosaur* means "terrible lizard."

What the colors and symbols mean

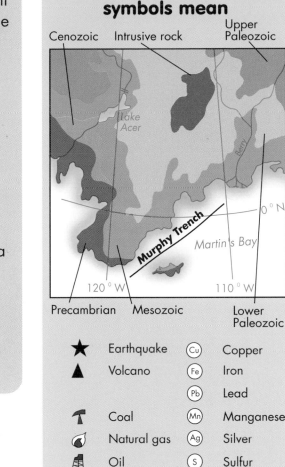

Cenozoic   Intrusive rock   Upper Paleozoic

Lake Acer

Murphy Trench

Martin's Bay

120 ° W   110 ° W

Precambrian   Mesozoic   Lower Paleozoic

★	Earthquake	Cu	Copper
▲	Volcano	Fe	Iron
		Pb	Lead
⛏	Coal	Mn	Manganese
🛢	Natural gas	Ag	Silver
⛽	Oil	S	Sulfur
U	Uranium	Sn	Tin
Al	Bauxite	Ti	Titanium
		Zn	Zinc

0   200   400 miles

? Did You Know

★ The largest gem cut from the Cullinan, a rough diamond, is called the "Star of Africa" and can be seen in the Tower of London in the Royal Sceptre.

★ An earthquake usually lasts for about 1 minute, but in 1755 an earthquake in Lisbon, Portugal, lasted for 10 minutes.

★ Neanderthal, close to Düsseldorf, Germany, is where the first skull of a Neanderthal man was discovered.

India and its immediate neighbors make up a Precambrian mini-continent, tacked on after the break up of Gondwanaland to the southern mountain region of Asia proper. The mostly flat, arid land produces large quantities of iron and bauxite.

Things to do

If you have any spare time, making a rock, mineral, and fossil collection can be fun. Before you go out to look you need to gather together some equipment.

Trowel

Notebook and pencil

Old brushes or toothbrush

Newspaper

Chisel

Small hammer

Helmet or hat to protect your head

Satchel

The hammer is useful to split open rocks and pebbles, the chisel to gently ease out fossils, and the brushes to clean off the dust. A notebook is useful to record your finds and the newspaper to wrap them up to take home. A hard hat is advised when looking for fossils and rocks in quarries or near cliffs.

Remember to always tell someone where you are going and check if it is safe for you to go there.

Formation of Igneous Rocks

The word *igneous* comes from the latin word *igneus,* meaning "fire." During volcanic eruptions, molten lava flows downhill. Houses, trees

Tropic of Cancer

Gulf of Kutch

20°N

Arabian Sea

10°N

70°E

Helmand

Indus

Chambal

Ganges

Krishna

Krishna

Gulf of Mannar

INDIAN OCEAN

d crops are burned and buried by
e advancing lava. The lava
rdens to form new igneous rocks,
t because lava destroys
erything it touches, this rock
es not contain fossils. It can be
vided into two main types:

trusive Igneous Rocks
eneath the hard outer layers of
e Earth is a layer of magma.
me magma rises through the
erlying rocks into the crust.
me of it accumulates in huge
eas called batholiths. Here it
ols and hardens slowly to form
arse-grained rocks containing

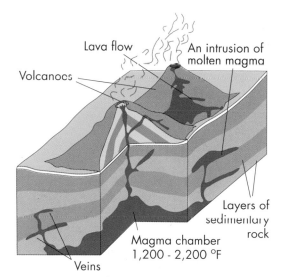

Lava flow
An intrusion of
molten magma
Volcanoes
Layers of
sedimentary
rock
Magma chamber
1,200 - 2,200 °F
Veins

sizable mineral crystals. Batholiths
often push up the overlying rocks to
form domes.

When the overlying rocks are worn
away, the rocks in the batholith
appear on the surface. These rocks
are called intrusive igneous rock.

Extrusive Igneous Rocks
These form from magma that
reaches the Earth's surface. Some
form when magma spills out as lava
through volcanoes or cracks in the
ground. The lava cools and hardens
quickly in the air. If magma is
forced to the surface quickly, there
is only enough time for small
crystals to form. Sometimes they
are so small they can only be seen
with a microscope. Basalt is the
most common extrusive igneous
rock. It is a very hard black rock
and feels rough and heavy.

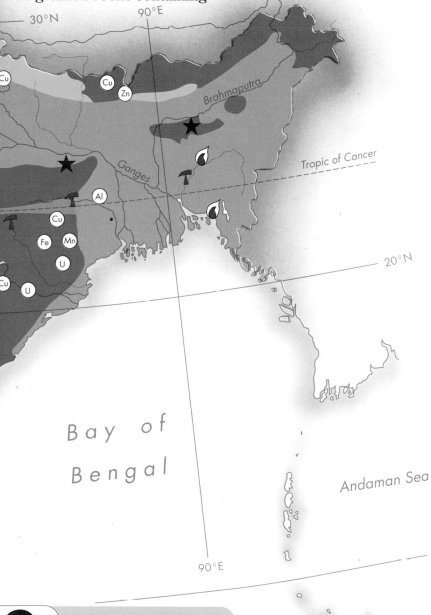

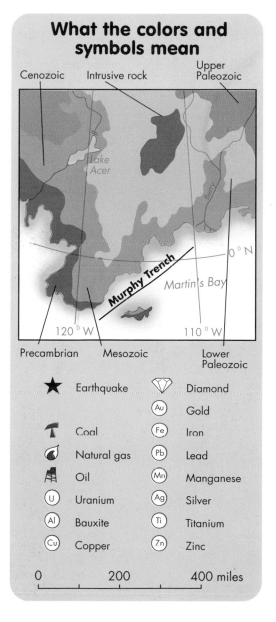

What the colors and symbols mean

Cenozoic   Intrusive rock   Upper Paleozoic

Lake Acer

Murphy Trench

Martin's Bay

0°N

120°W   110°W

Precambrian   Mesozoic   Lower Paleozoic

★ Earthquake	◇ Diamond
⊤ Coal	(Au) Gold
Natural gas	(Fe) Iron
Oil	(Pb) Lead
(U) Uranium	(Mn) Manganese
(Al) Bauxite	(Ag) Silver
(Cu) Copper	(Ti) Titanium
	(Zn) Zinc

0   200   400 miles

? Did You Know

★ The Early Ape, first hominid
humanlike) fossil, was discovered
India and named for Rama, a
anifestation of God.

This portion of the globe is sitting on a small ocean of "black gold" — oil. Over half of the world's oil reserves are located in this geographic region.

Formation of Oil and Natural Gas

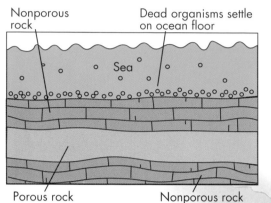

Nonporous rock

Dead organisms settle on ocean floor

Sea

Porous rock

Nonporous rock

Oil and natural gas were formed millions of years ago. Tiny plants and animals that lived in shallow water died and sank to the bottom. They decomposed into a dark, slimy ooze. Layers of mud, deposited by rivers, covered the decomposed plants and animals. With the heat and pressure of the sediments on top, the dark, slimy ooze turned into oil and natural gas.

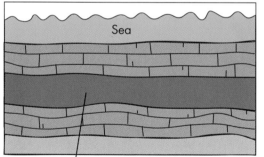

Sea

Porous rock containing oil, natural gas, and water

The oil and gas then seeped through layers of porous rock until they came up against a more solid rock and were trapped. They accumulated at the top of folded rock strata or at the sides of salt domes that had thrust themselves up through the strata from deep underground.

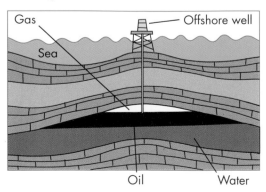

Gas

Offshore well

Sea

Oil

Water

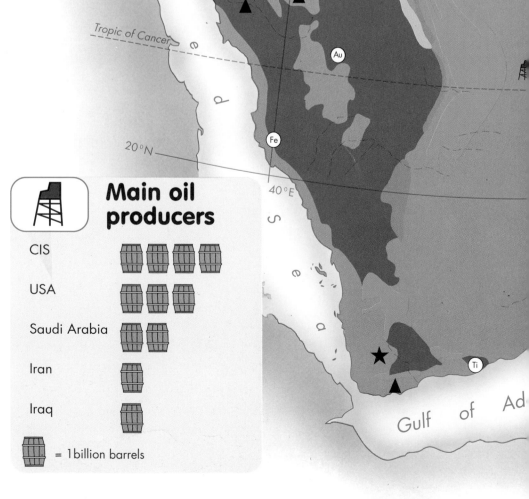

Black Sea

North Anatolian Transform Fault

East Anatolian Transform Fault

Mediterranean Sea

Tigris

Lake Van

Euphrates

Tigris

Euphrates

Tropic of Cancer

30°N

20°N

30°E

40°N

30°E

40°E

30°E

40°E

Main oil producers

CIS	🛢️🛢️🛢️🛢️
USA	🛢️🛢️🛢️
Saudi Arabia	🛢️🛢️
Iran	🛢️
Iraq	🛢️

🛢️ = 1 billion barrels

Gulf of Ad

Red Sea

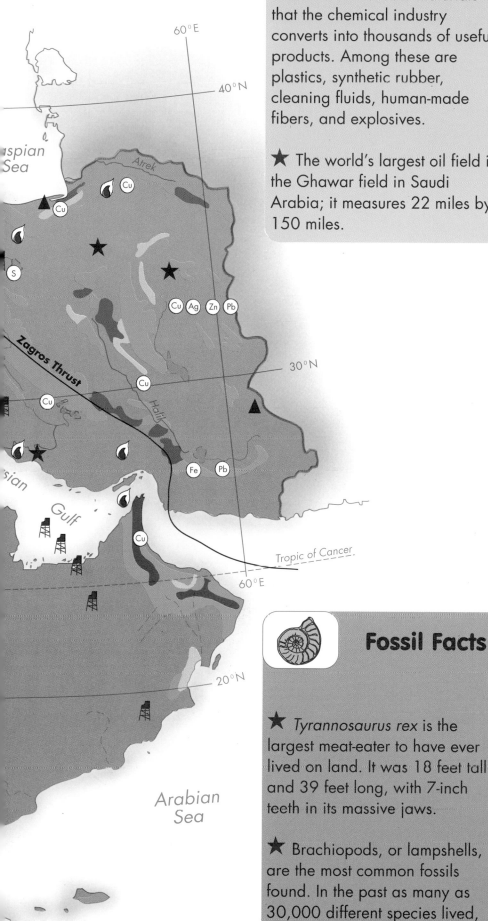

★ Oil is more than just a fuel. It is a reservoir of raw materials that the chemical industry converts into thousands of useful products. Among these are plastics, synthetic rubber, cleaning fluids, human-made fibers, and explosives.

★ The world's largest oil field is the Ghawar field in Saudi Arabia; it measures 22 miles by 150 miles.

! Amazing – But True

★ Underneath the tiny country of Kuwait is roughly 10% of the world's oil supply.

★ Pound-for-pound, oil has about one and a half times the heating value of coal.

What the colors and symbols mean

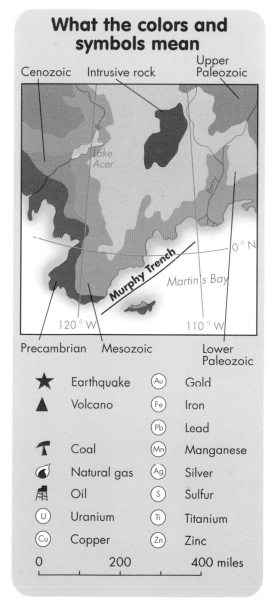

Cenozoic Intrusive rock Upper Paleozoic

Lake Acer

Bercy

Murphy Trench

0° N

Martin's Bay

120° W   110° W

Precambrian Mesozoic Lower Paleozoic

★	Earthquake	Ⓐᵤ	Gold
▲	Volcano	Ⓕₑ	Iron
		Ⓟᵦ	Lead
⛏	Coal	Ⓜₙ	Manganese
🛢	Natural gas	Ⓐg	Silver
🛢	Oil	Ⓢ	Sulfur
Ⓤ	Uranium	Ⓣᵢ	Titanium
Ⓒᵤ	Copper	Ⓩₙ	Zinc

0   200   400 miles

🐚 Fossil Facts

★ *Tyrannosaurus rex* is the largest meat-eater to have ever lived on land. It was 18 feet tall and 39 feet long, with 7-inch teeth in its massive jaws.

★ Brachiopods, or lampshells, are the most common fossils found. In the past as many as 30,000 different species lived, but today only about 300 species can be found in the seas.

Not so much a continent, Oceania is the name now given to a vast area of ocean dotted with islands, spreading from Australasia in the western Pacific to South America.

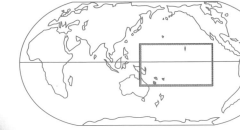

PACIFIC

OCEAN

Marianas Trench

Micronesia

Melanesia

10°N

Equator

0°

10°S

Arafura Sea

Gulf of Papua

Solomon Sea

Solomon South Solomon Trench

New Hebrides Trench

Coral Sea

20°S

140°E

150°E

160°E

170°E

140°E

150°E

160°E

170°E

Tropic of Capricorn

30°S

Al

Au

?

Did You Know

★ Each year 20 to 30 volcanoes erupt. The largest active volcano on earth is Mauna Loa in Hawaii.

What the colors and symbols mean

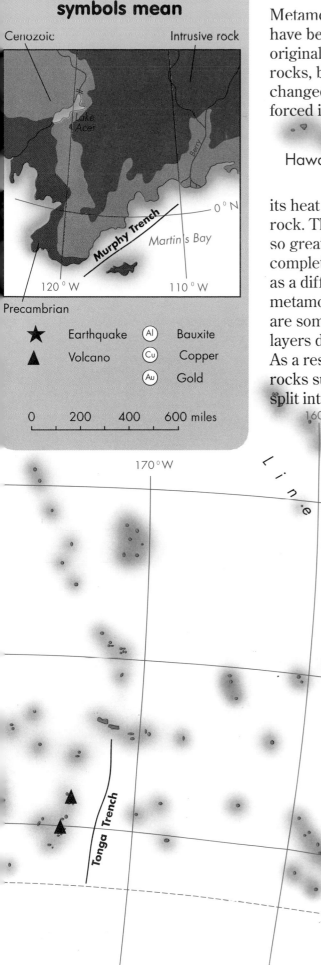

Cenozoic

Intrusive rock

Lake Acer

Berry

Murphy Trench

0°N

Martin's Bay

120°W

110°W

Precambrian

★ Earthquake   (Al) Bauxite

▲ Volcano   (Cu) Copper

            (Au) Gold

0   200   400   600 miles

Formation of Metamorphic Rocks

Metamorphic rocks are rocks that have been changed. They were originally igneous or sedimentary rocks, but heat and pressure have changed them. Molten magma gets forced into sedimentary rocks, and

Hawaii

Mauna Loa

its heat cooks the surrounding rock. The heat and pressure can be so great that the original rock is completely melted and recrystalizes as a different rock — a metamorphic rock. The molecules are sometimes rearranged into layers due to the pressure and heat. As a result some metamorphosed rocks such as slate can be easily split into thin sheets.

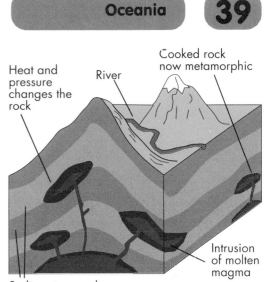

Cooked rock now metamorphic

Heat and pressure changes the rock

River

Intrusion of molten magma

Sedimentary rock

Usually the new rocks are much harder than the original rocks. Metamorphic rocks are also formed by the pressure caused when they are squeezed together by the movement of the Earth's crust. Sometimes minerals in metamorphic rocks are recrystalized to form new minerals. Garnets, used in jewelry, are crystals often found in schists (pronounced shist) and gneisses (pronounced nice) and are created during metamorphism.

160°W

150°W

170°W

Line Islands

Equator

0°

Polynesia

140°W

130°W

10°S

Tonga Trench

20°S

Tropic of Capricorn

130°W

170°W

160°W

150°W

30°S

140°W

Geologically, the country is composed of the older Precambrian rock formations of the eastern and central regions. These give way to the newer Mesozoic and Cenozoic mountain regions of the western region and Pacific coastline.

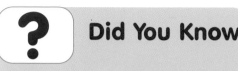

? Did You Know

★ Yellowstone Park in the USA has hot springs and 10,000 geysers. The geyser called Old Faithful erupts to a height of 130 feet every 30 minutes.

★ The world's tallest oil production platform stands in water that is 1,760 feet deep and is in place 100 miles off the Louisiana coast.

★ Earthquakes mostly occur at the plate edges, especially where plates collide, push into each other, or slide past one another, as at the San Andreas fault in California.

★ The largest crocodile lived 75 million years ago in what is now Texas. It was 52 feet in length.

★ There is a Dinosaur National Museum in Utah. Here a 190-foot wall has more than a thousand dinosaur bones embedded in it. This wall was once part of a sandy river bed in which dinosaurs became stuck and died.

★ The town of Artesia in Colorado changed its name to Dinosaur because so many dinosaur fossils were found nearby. Even the streets are named for dinosaurs.

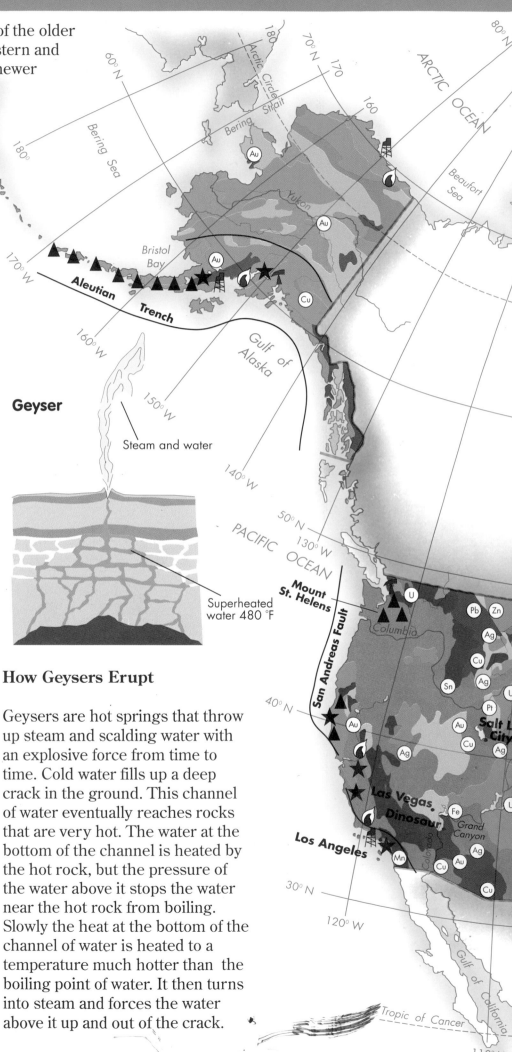

Geyser

Steam and water

Superheated water 480 °F

How Geysers Erupt

Geysers are hot springs that throw up steam and scalding water with an explosive force from time to time. Cold water fills up a deep crack in the ground. This channel of water eventually reaches rocks that are very hot. The water at the bottom of the channel is heated by the hot rock, but the pressure of the water above it stops the water near the hot rock from boiling. Slowly the heat at the bottom of the channel of water is heated to a temperature much hotter than the boiling point of water. It then turns into steam and forces the water above it up and out of the crack.

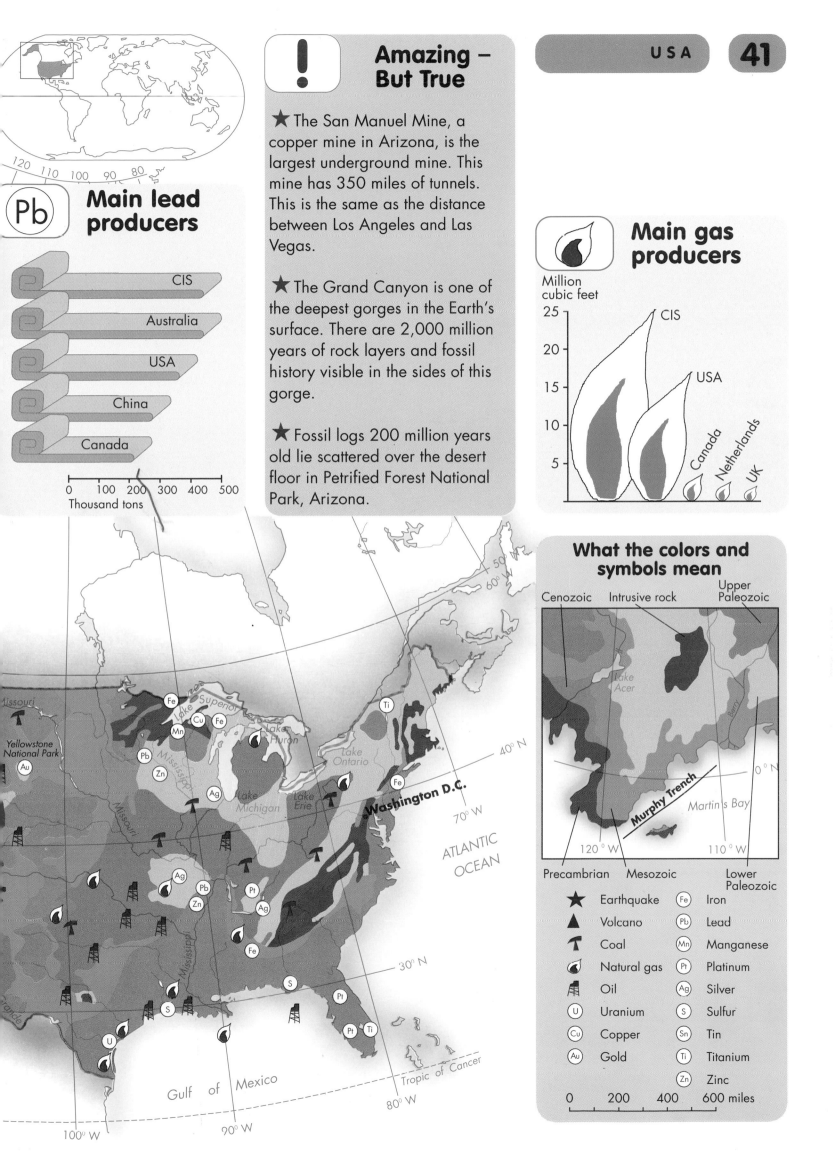

Pb Main lead producers

CIS
Australia
USA
China
Canada

0 100 200 300 400 500
Thousand tons

Amazing – But True

★ The San Manuel Mine, a copper mine in Arizona, is the largest underground mine. This mine has 350 miles of tunnels. This is the same as the distance between Los Angeles and Las Vegas.

★ The Grand Canyon is one of the deepest gorges in the Earth's surface. There are 2,000 million years of rock layers and fossil history visible in the sides of this gorge.

★ Fossil logs 200 million years old lie scattered over the desert floor in Petrified Forest National Park, Arizona.

Main gas producers

Million cubic feet

25
20
15
10
5

CIS
USA
Canada
Netherlands
UK

What the colors and symbols mean

Cenozoic   Intrusive rock   Upper Paleozoic

Lake Acer

Berry

Murphy Trench   Martin's Bay

120° W   110° W

Precambrian   Mesozoic   Lower Paleozoic

★	Earthquake	Fe	Iron
▲	Volcano	Pb	Lead
⊤	Coal	Mn	Manganese
🜂	Natural gas	Pt	Platinum
⛏	Oil	Ag	Silver
U	Uranium	S	Sulfur
Cu	Copper	Sn	Tin
Au	Gold	Ti	Titanium
		Zn	Zinc

0   200   400   600 miles

Missouri
Fe
Lake Superior
Cu Fe
Mn
Lake Huron
Ti

Yellowstone National Park
Au
Pb
Zn
Lake Michigan
Ag
Lake Ontario
Lake Erie
Fe
Washington D.C.
40° N
70° W
ATLANTIC OCEAN

Missouri
Ag
Pb
Zn
Pt
Ag
Fe
30° N

Mississippi
S
Pt
U
S
Pt Ti

Gulf of Mexico
Tropic of Cancer
80° W
90° W
100° W

120 110 100 90 80

Ammonite
An extinct marine mollusc with a coiled and partitioned shell. It was common in Mesozoic times.

Amphibian
A cold–blooded creature with a backbone. Generally, amphibians live on the land and breed in the water; examples are frogs, newts, and toads.

Batholith
A dome–shaped mass of igneous rock, especially granite, formed from an intrusion of magma at great depth.

Brachiopod
A marine creature with a shell from which threadlike feeding organs project.

Caldera
A large, basin–shaped crater bounded by steep cliffs, usually formed by the collapse of the top of a volcano. It may contain a lake.

Continental drift
The theory that the earth's continents move gradually over the surface of the planet on a bed of magma.

Core
The central part of the earth; about 4,300 miles in diameter.

Crust
Outer layer of the earth, between 3 and 25 miles thick.

Echinoid
Sea urchin.

Evolution
Gradual change in the characteristics of a population of plants or animals over successive generations.

Fossil
The remains or the form of an animal or plant that has been preserved embedded in the rocks of the earth's crust.

Gneiss
Coarse–grained metamorphic rock that is banded into crude layers of dark and light minerals.

Graptolite
An extinct Paleozoic creature; graptolites lived in colonies, and their fossils can be found in ample numbers.

Hominoid
Humanlike; part of the primate family, which includes some apes and all humans.

Magma
The molten material that exists beneath the solid layer of rock that forms the earth's crust.

Mantle
The part of the earth between the crust and the core; made up of rocks of a higher density than those of the crust.

Peninsula
A narrow strip of land, projecting into a sea or lake, and almost surrounded by water.

Petrified
The change of organic material into fossilized form by impregnation with dissolved minerals, so that its form is preserved.

Porous
Able to absorb water or other fluids.

Schist
A metamorphic rock that can be split into many thin plates. Formed by the effects of intense heat and pressure.

Strata
The distinct layers into which sedimentary rocks can be divided.

Trench
A deep, elongated trough in the floor of the ocean.

Trilobites
Extinct marine creatures, common during the Paleozoic era, which had an external skeleton divided into three parts.

Vent
The shaft of a volcano through which lava and gases erupt.

Viscous
Thick and sticky.

Barnes-Svarney, Patricia L. *Born of Heat and Pressure: Mountains and Metamorphic Rocks.*
Hillside, NJ: Enslow, 1991.

———. *Clocks in the Rocks: Learning About Earth's Past.*
Hillside, NJ: Enslow, 1991.

Dixon, Dougal. *Geology.*
New York: Watts, 1982.

Energlyn, William David Evans. Baron, *Through the Crust of the Earth.*
New York: McGraw-Hill, 1973.

Gallant, Roy A. *Our Restless Earth.*
New York: Watts, 1986.

Klaits, Barrie. *When You Find a Rock: A Field Guide.*
New York: Macmillan, 1976.

Lambert, David. *Rocks and Minerals.*
New York: Watts, 1986.

McGowen, Tom. *Album of Rocks and Minerals.*
Chicago: Rand McNally, 1981.

Selsam, Millicent. *A First Look at Rocks.*
New York: Walker, 1984.

This index is designed to help you to find places shown on the maps. The index is in alphabetical order and lists all towns, countries, and physical features. After each entry extra information is given to describe the entry and to tell you which country or continent it is in.

The next column contains the latitude and longitude figures. These are used to help locate places on maps. They are measured in degrees. The blue lines drawn across the map are lines of latitude. The equator is at latitude 0°. All lines above the equator are referred to as °N (north of the equator). All lines below the equator are referred to as °S (south of the equator).

The blue lines drawn from the top to the bottom of the map are lines of longitude. The 0° line passes through Greenwich, London, and is known as the Greenwich Meridian. All lines of longitude join the North Pole to the South Pole. All lines to the right of the Greenwich Meridian are referred to as °E (east of Greenwich), and all lines to the left of the Greenwich Meridian are referred to as °W (west of Greenwich).

The final column indicates the number of the page where you will find the place for which you are searching.

If you want to find out where the Gulf of Thailand is, look it up in the alphabetical index. The entry will read:

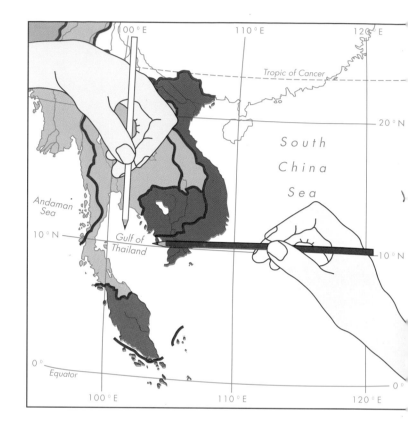

Name, Description	Location		Page
	Lat.	Long.	
Thailand, Gulf of, Asia	11°N	101°E	22

Turn to page 22 in your atlas. The Gulf of Thailand is located where latitude 11°N meets longitude 101°E. Place a pencil along latitude 11°N. Now take another pencil and place it along 101°E. Where the two pencils meet is the location of the Gulf of Thailand. Practice finding places in the index and on the maps.

Scott E. Morris is an associate professor of geography at the University of Idaho, where his current areas of teaching and research interest include mountain geomorphology, field methods, and human impact on the landscape process. Dr. Morris received his Ph.D. from the University of Colorado, Boulder, and has published prolifically on the formation and climatic history of mountain landscapes, the effects of wildfire and mineral resource extraction on soil erosion processes, and the influence of water diversion and channel modification on sediment transport.